The American Experiment in Ordered Liberty

John C. Pinheiro

D0108221

ACTONINSTITUTE

Christian Social Thought Series
Number 26 • Edited by Kevin Schmiesing

Christian Social Thought Series, Number 26

© 2019 by Acton Institute

Acton Institute
for the Study of Religion and Liberty
All rights reserved.

Cover image: Declaration and American Flag
Source: www.istock.com

ISBN: 978-1-880595-12-1

Interior composition: Judy Schafer
Cover: Peter Ho

ACTONINSTITUTE

98 E. Fulton
Grand Rapids, Michigan 49503
616.454.3080
www.acton.org

Printed in the United States of America

Contents

Foreword

The longstanding and much-debated question of whether and to what extent Catholicism is compatible with the American project remains contentious. The question is closely tied to other, not-quite-synonymous ones, which take us beyond the United States to areas of concern to Christians in many national and cultural contexts: Is Catholicism compatible with democracy? Is it compatible with capitalism? With separation of church and state?

In our own time there is once again a strong movement toward answering such questions in the negative. Unlike previous episodes in American history, much of the push comes not from anti-Catholic bigots who wish to deny papists a place in a Protestant or a secular society, but instead from writers and intellectuals who are themselves Catholics. Disillusioned with the failure of the Church in America to create a vibrant, orthodox, radically Christian faith community, they place blame on the acids of modernity that permeate American culture and on Catholics for failing to recognize and protect themselves from those corrosive influences. We have been too much *in* the world, they say, and have become *of* it.

Insofar as that critique makes the Catholic encounter with American culture, politics, and economy more realistic and more securely grounded in Christian theology and praxis, it is a salutary movement. The temptation to confuse or conflate the City of God and the City of Man is constant, and eternal vigilance is the price of (genuine Christian) liberty.

But there is also a danger in the tendency to find threat rather than promise in the American project: the possibility of throwing the proverbial baby out with the bathwater. The weaknesses in American culture must be weighed against its strengths. A theoretical ideal is not a fair measure of American accomplishments in building a society based on justice, truth, and freedom. It is better to compare the American experiment in ordered liberty with other cultures and nations that have actually existed.

In this volume, Professor John Pinheiro brings historical expertise to the topic, assessing the merits of the American project by focusing on the founding period. He examines the views of the founders and the realities of early American culture in light of the principles of Catholic social teaching and finds no clear and simple answer to the question of Catholic and American compatibility. What he does conclude, however—and it is important—is that viewing America (or the founding) in ideological terms is a mistake. The American experiment was not at the outset the realization of an ideological agenda; instead, it was the practical outworking of a commitment to protect the liberties to which Americans believed themselves due. These liberties were, at least in large measure, consistent with or even derived from Catholic principles concerning the nature of the human person and social relations.

If the American project is not perfect, neither is it beyond redemption. Pinheiro points out that the task given to Catholics is not, in a fit of despair, to raze the institutions of religious and political liberty (who knows what might take their place?), but instead to "redeem the time" by embracing what is good and discouraging what is bad in the current state of affairs. Pinheiro is a wise guide to discerning between the two as Christians—in America and across the world—seek a path forward in charity and truth.

Kevin Schmiesing
Acton Institute

Introduction

Finding "Freedom's Fulfillment in the Truth"

"America," proclaimed Pope St. John Paul II at an American ballpark in 1995, "has always wanted to be a land of the free. Today, the challenge facing America is to find freedom's fulfillment in the truth." In the wake of the end of the Cold War and the demise of the Soviet Union, this question had a particular saliency for Americans in the 1990s. Had they "won" the Cold War? And if so, what had they won? Was there a purpose, even a providential one, in their victory? This question of freedom in truth and what to do with one's freedom had long been a special challenge for Catholic Americans. The United States of America was a country born in revolution during the Enlightenment, often speaking the languages of liberalism and Protestant Christianity at the same time. While popes condemned this liberalism, American Protestants argued that Catholics were unable to participate in a democratic polity because their faith was inimical to civil and religious liberty. By its very nature, they argued, Catholicism was incompatible with democracy.[1]

---

1 John Paul II, Homily at Camden Yards, Baltimore, Maryland, 8 October 1995, https://w2.vatican.va/content/john-paul-ii/en/ homilies /1995 /documents/hf_jp-ii_hom_19951008_baltimore. html.

John Paul II was aware of this history when it came to American freedom and the Catholic faith. In his short but profound homily, he pressed further on what he meant by finding "freedom's fulfillment in the truth." The question of this fulfillment had occupied two previous popes, Pius IX and Gregory XVI (both men of the early to mid-nineteenth century), each of whom had in specific contexts condemned liberalism and certain freedoms on which Americans placed great value. Late in the nineteenth century, Pope Leo XIII condemned what he called "Americanism," a censure that had a greater impact on European Catholics than it did on Catholic Americans. But John Paul had not come to Baltimore to condemn Americans. He had come to challenge them. "We must guard the truth that is the condition of authentic freedom, the truth that allows freedom to be fulfilled in goodness."

To what sort of truth was John Paul referring? "The truth," said John Paul, "that is intrinsic to human life created in God's image and likeness, the truth that is written on the human heart, the truth that can be known by reason and can therefore form the basis of a profound and universal dialogue among people about the direction they must give to their lives and their activities." He boiled it down to truths about God and truths about the human person. "Sometimes, witnessing to Christ will mean drawing out of a culture the full meaning of its noblest intentions, a fullness that is revealed in Christ. At other times, witnessing to Christ means challenging that culture, especially when the truth about the human person is under assault."[2]

"The basic question before a democratic society," John Paul went on to say, is "how ought we to live together?" The question of how one ought to live is among the oldest questions of mankind. Democracy adds to this, John Paul claimed, because we citizens have our own determinative role to play toward

---

2   John Paul II, Homily at Camden Yards.

the common good. John Paul appealed to President Abraham Lincoln to answer this question about American democracy. During the Civil War, Lincoln had argued that America's real roots were to be found in the claim that "All men are created equal." America did have a founding, thought Lincoln, and its most important founding claim—one that preceded the Articles of Confederation as well as the US Constitution—was to be found in Thomas Jefferson's Declaration of Independence. G. K. Chesterton argues that Jefferson in the Declaration "dogmatically bases all rights on the fact that God created all men equal.... There is no basis for democracy except in a dogma about the divine origin of man."[3]

It was in Lincoln's argument that John Paul found the answer for late twentieth-century American soul-searching. Importantly, this answer turned out to be the same Christian anthropology proposed by the Catholic Church: "President Lincoln's question is no less a question for the present generation of Americans. Democracy cannot be sustained without *a shared commitment to certain moral truths about the human person and human community.*" In words that echoed Lord Acton's, John Paul reminded Americans that "freedom consists not in doing what we like, but in having the right to do what we ought."[4]

The truths about the human person and thus also about the "human community" that are present to some degree in the words of Jefferson and Lincoln are seen at their fullest in

---

3 John Paul II, Homily at Camden Yards; G. K. Chesterton, *What I Saw in America* (New York: Dodd, Mead, and Co., 1922), reprint, G. K. Chesterton: *Collected Works*, 37 vols. (San Francisco: Ignatius Press, 1990), 21:261.

4 John Paul II, Homily at Camden Yards. See Lord Acton, "The Church in the Modern World," in *Essays in Religion, Politics, and Morality*, vol. 3, ed. J. Rufus Fears (Indianapolis: Liberty Classics, 1985), 613.

Catholic social teaching (CST). This is why Chesterton refer-red to democracy as "mystical democracy" and why he argued that as long as the American democracy "becomes or remains Catholic and Christian, that democracy will remain demo-cratic. Insofar as it does not, it will become wildly and wickedly undemocratic."[5] Catholic social teaching, as it has developed since Pope Leo XIII's encyclical, *Rerum Novarum*, is rooted in three assumptions about the human person and natural law: (1) The human person has transcendent value; (2) because of this the good of the person cannot be subordinated to other goods; and (3) it follows that social structures, governmental or otherwise, must either be ordered to this good or at least not interfere with it. The Catholic Church teaches that the ultimate purpose and final end, or *telos*, of the human person is to know, love, and serve God. This is revealed truth, unknowable through other means, including reason. This is the truth that sets one free. This revelation of truth means that all human relationships ought to be ordered according to love.[6]

---

[5] Chesterton, *What I Saw in America*, 21:263.

[6] I am indebted here to my Aquinas College colleague, Stephan Davis, who has dubbed these the "three root assumptions of CST." The Catholic bishops of the United States identify seven themes: Life and Dignity of the Human Person; Call to Family, Community, and Participation; Rights and Responsibilities; Option for the Poor and Vulnerable; The Dignity of Work and the Rights of Workers; Solidarity; and Care for God's Creation. Any list like this might imply equality among the teachings but in fact there is a discern-able moral hierarchy among them, descending from the Catholic understanding of the dignity of the person. The *Compendium of the Social Doctrine of the Church*, issued by the Pontifical Council for Justice and Peace, gives four "permanent principles" of the Church's social doctrine: the dignity of the human person, the common good, subsidiarity, and solidarity. United States Conference of Catholic Bishops (USCCB), "Seven Themes of Catholic Social

Is the American political order compatible with Catholicism? The answer rests on what "compatibility" means. No political order is fully compatible with Catholicism or the Christian dispensation but heaven—not even that great civilization called Christendom that produced Dante, St. Francis of Assisi, and St. Thomas Aquinas. John Paul clearly found great promise in America, in its democracy, in its religious freedom, and in the claims made by Lincoln regarding human equality.

John Paul knew that to talk of compatibility with democracy is not to approve every decision the *demos* makes, any more than our freedom of the will means God approves every decision we make. Neither was Thomas Aquinas making a case for anarchy when he argued that not everything that is immoral should be illegal. Nor was he arguing for religious indifference when he wrote of tolerating non-Christian rites "either on account of some good that ensues therefrom, or because of some evil avoided."[7] Religious toleration was not a creation of Enlightenment liberals or of *Dignitatis Humanae*. It had a long heritage in the American colonies and the early republic. "This principle," Russell Kirk points out, "owed almost nothing to the theories of the Enlightenment, then popular in France."[8] It also was long a part of the Catholic tradition, even when

---

Teaching," http://www.usccb.org/beliefs-and-teachings/what-we-believe/catholic-social-teaching/seven-themes-of-catholic-social-teaching.cfm; Pontifical Council for Justice and Peace, *Compendium of the Social Doctrine of the Church* (2004), chap. 4, http://www.vatican.va/roman_curia/pontifical_councils/justpeace/documents/rc_pc_justpeace_doc_20060526_compendio-dott-soc_en.html.

7   Thomas Aquinas, *Summa Theologiae*, II-II, 10, 11.

8   Russell Kirk, *The Roots of American Order* (1974; reprint, Wilmington: ISI Books, 2003), 437.

not practiced.[9] As we will see, the history of the United States played a key role in the development of the magisterial teaching on religious liberty that produced *Dignitatis Humanae*.

The Catholic Church gives no prescription for a political order for Christians.[10] Christianity has flourished under deep oppression (Rome before 313, for example), and it has atrophied in states where Crown and Altar were unified, including in the Papal States. Saint Augustine of Hippo argued that the true end of the City of Man is the maintenance of peace and perpetuation of justice on earth. As a good, this is in agreement with the highest good of mankind, the City of God. The state's most appropriate role is to ward against the various forces of destruction so that people might be free to reach their end in God. Saint Augustine writes about the pilgrim church amid the earth's plurality of civilizations:

> This heavenly city, then, while it sojourns on earth, calls
> citizens out of all nations, and gathers together a society
> of pilgrims of all languages, not scrupling about diver-
> sities in manners, laws, and institutions. It therefore is
> so far from rescinding and abolishing these diversities,
> that it even preserves and adapts them, so long only as

---

9 See Robert Louis Wilken, *Liberty in the Things of God: The Christian Origins of Religious Freedom* (New Haven: Yale University
   Press, 2019).

10 "Since it is not an ideology, the Christian faith does not presume to
    imprison changing socio-political realities in a rigid schema, and it
    recognizes that human life is realized in history in conditions that
    are diverse and imperfect. Furthermore, in constantly reaffirming
    the transcendent dignity of the person, the Church's method is
    always that of respect for freedom." John Paul II, Encyclical Letter
    Centesimus Annus (1991), no. 46.

no hindrance to the worship of the one supreme and true God is thus introduced.[11]

In *Democracy in America*, Alexis de Tocqueville draws on St. Augustine to argue that "if the human mind is allowed to follow its own bent, it will regulate political society and the City of God in the same uniform manner and will, I dare say, seek to *harmonize* earth and Heaven."[12] If I am created free in order to seek and know the truth, how am I supposed to live and what ought society look like?

This book gets at this compatibility question by focusing on the founding years of the republic. We first need to determine whether America really was founded on a creed. Was America doomed to fail from its inception because it had a "hard" founding rooted in a poisonous, false anthropology? Do the "culture of death" and what Pope Francis calls a "throwaway culture" owe their existence not to human sin and the ascent of a post-Christian vision of progress but rather to a small set of faulty ideas instantiated in the body politic by the Founding Fathers? Conversely, as John Courtney Murray argued, did the founders "build better than they knew," drawing not on individualistic rights and Jacobin radicalism for their creed but rather on their own experience and a natural law discernable through reason with clear links to the Catholic tradition?[13] Finally, what if there was no hard founding at all—no consciously wrought creed, as such—but rather the preservation and codification of ancient

---

11 Augustine of Hippo, *City of God*, chapter 17, https://www.ccel.org /ccel/schaff/npnf102.iv.XIX.17.html.

12 Alexis de Tocqueville, *Democracy in America*, trans. Gerald E. Bevan (1835–1840; New York: Penguin Books, 2003), 336.

13 Murray takes the language of "building better than they knew" from the American bishops' statement at the Third Plenary Council of Baltimore (1884).

traditions with links to the classical and Christian worlds? Late eighteenth-century America was a time when civic republicanism meshed healthily in tension with Christian teaching, the desire for virtue, and nearly two centuries of English colonial experience. To paraphrase St. John Paul, we want to find out whether the American experiment is an experiment in *freedom only* or an experiment of *freedom in truth*.

1 America: "A Nation with the Soul of a Church"?*

For over five hundred years, the world's greatest thinkers and scholars have struggled to discover just how new the New World is. The United States of America has drawn particular attention, because it was founded in the name of liberty and through revolution during the eighteenth-century European Enlightenments.

The United States was the first large republic since ancient Rome. English intellectuals ranging from Charles Dickens and Lord Acton to G. K. Chesterton visited the United States in the nineteenth and early twentieth centuries, hoping to uncover the sources of American prosperity and freedom. We misunderstand this interest in America if we think it was merely one of ideological politics or the curiosity of dilettantes. These intellectuals sought meaning in America. They wanted to know just what made Americans tick. They hoped to measure the degree to which the liberties they enjoyed were particular to Americans and the degree to which these things might be realized as universal goods.

The intertwined histories of England and the United States, including the fact that the American political, legal, and moral heritage is overwhelmingly British, make this English curiosity easy to understand. (Even so, Chesterton actually found

---

* G. K. Chesterton, *What I Saw in America*, 45.

Americans to be more European than British.) The most astute observer of American democracy, however, was not an Englishman but the French aristocrat, Alexis de Tocqueville. Tocqueville's *Democracy in America*, published in the 1830s, remains the best book not only on American democracy but also on democracy itself. Indeed, Tocqueville's book is as much about what it means to be human as it is about any political system or way of life. Like J. Hector St. John de Crèvecœur, who had toured the United States in the 1780s, Tocqueville wanted to know what made the American republic successful in spite of the degenerate effects natural to democracy. The answer, he decided, lay in religion and religious liberty.

Even as liberal revolutions during the nineteenth century repeatedly failed in Europe and in the Americas, the United States thrived, prospered, and grew. It did so even in spite of a bloody civil war in the 1860s. This anomaly, too, made it an object of study. European revolutions seemed bent on the destruction of society and of religion. Visitors to the United States quickly found that these impulses were almost nonexistent among Americans. Indeed, in *The Old Regime and the Revolution*, Tocqueville credited Americans' "respect for religion" as "the greatest guarantee of the state's stability and the safety of individuals." Americans had prudently not adopted *in toto* what Tocqueville calls "the boldest political doctrines of theories of eighteenth-century philosophers." Instead, while there was no other country where these doctrines "could be more rigorously instituted than in America [such] anti-religious doctrines exclusively have never been able to see the light of day in America, even on behalf of the unlimited liberty of the press." According to William B. Allen, "Tocqueville means that Americans adopted these theories up to a point but stopped, whereas the French did not stop" but instead "attacked religion ferociously."[1]

The one question that most occupied thoughtful observers where America was concerned was, how am I supposed to live? Perhaps lessons could be found, for good or ill, in the ways in which Americans lived, worked, worshiped, and interacted with each other. As Chesterton put it, he came to America "to inquire what it really is which makes America peculiar, or which is peculiar to America. In short ... to get some ultimate idea of what America *is*; and the answer to that question will reveal something much deeper and grander and more worthy of our intelligent interest."[2] As with Tocqueville and others before him, he was sure there was meaning to be found, but what was it?

This thinking on America is best divided into two broad schools of thought. Chesterton laid out the first of these when he toured the United States in 1921 and again in 1930. He brought with him his sensibilities as both an Englishman and a Catholic, officially joining the Catholic Church one year after his first visit. He wrote one book for each trip: *What I Saw in America* (1922) and *Sidelights on New London and Newer York* (1932).[3] Along with these came the many columns he wrote during his visits for the *Illustrated London News*.

---

1   William B. Allen, "Radical Challenges to Liberal Democracy," in *Toward the Renewal of Civilization*, ed. T. William Boxx and Gary M. Quinlivan (Grand Rapids: Eerdmans, 1998), 77. The Tocqueville quotation comes from this page as well.

2   Chesterton, *What I Saw in America*, 41.

3   From his time in America, Charles Dickens produced one of his greatest novels, *Martin Chuzzlewit* (1842–1844), and *American Notes for General Circulation* (1842). Lord Acton's American journal from 1853 was published as *Acton in America* by Patmos Press in 1979.

In *What I Saw in America*, Chesterton wrote:

> America is the only nation in the world that is founded
> on a creed. That creed is set forth with dogmatic and even
> theological lucidity in the Declaration of Independence;
> perhaps the only piece of practical politics that is also
> theoretical politics and also great literature. It enunci-
> ates that all men are equal in their claim to justice, that
> governments exist to give them that justice, and that their
> authority for that reason is just. It certainly does condemn
> anarchism, and it does also by inference condemn athe-
> ism, since it clearly names the Creator as the ultimate
> authority from whom these equal rights are derived.[4]

America, according to Chesterton, had a *founding*, a well-
documented moment in time wherein a nation was created. This
founding, Chesterton argued, occurred on the basis of specific
ideas about justice, equality, and the human person.

John Courtney Murray agreed with Chesterton about what
the Jesuit called the "American Proposition." Murray admitted
that in the twentieth century the equality of human persons was
no longer self-evident and could be questioned. Yet he argued
in *We Hold These Truths* that "the American Proposition rests
on the forthright assertion of a realist epistemology": In other
words, universal truths about mankind that are discernable
through reason formed the foundation of American society
and government—what John Paul II in his 1995 Camden Yards
homily referred to as "the truth that can be known by reason
and can therefore form the basis of a profound and universal
dialogue."[5] How different this is than a culture and society
rooted in positivistic hypotheses, utilitarian calculations, idyl-
lic dreams, or ideological claims. "If this assertion is denied,"

---

[4]   Chesterton, *What I Saw in America*, 41.
[5]   John Paul II, Homily at Camden Yards.

Murray wrote, "the American Proposition is, I think, eviscerated at one stroke."[6]

Francis Cardinal George criticizes Murray for his "agnostic solution" of too strictly separating religion and politics. Murray, says George, quoting him, sees the two phrases of the First Amendment "not as 'articles of faith' but as 'articles of peace.'" They are political, not theological, and in Murray's mind this means that they make no claims on Catholics who in any case are called to transform any culture in which they live. This is "a neo-scholastic two-tiered conception of nature and grace" out of the "Suarezian Jesuit tradition." George thinks it is too sharp in its "delineation between the natural and the supernatural." If such a bald demarcation is true of the American founding, George is right to argue that this would undermine freedom and produce what John Paul called a "culture of death." "Without correlation to truths rooted in nature and in God," argues George, echoing John Paul, "human freedom becomes license or, alternatively, acquiesces in state tyranny."[7]

Where George sees a rupture, Murray sees development. Murray argues that Americans of the founding era *did* believe in a transcendent order and the existence of knowable truths. Once known, these truths could be integrated into society so that men might "dwell in dignity, peace, unity, justice, wellbeing, freedom." Indeed, they already were doing so by the 1760s. Between 1775 and 1783, Americans fought a revolution to preserve this free society in the face of a creeping tyranny. These truths about the human person buttressed American

---

6 John Courtney Murray, *We Hold These Truths: Catholic Reflections on the American Proposition* (Kansas City: Sheed and Ward, 1960), viii–ix.

7 Frances Cardinal George, *The Difference God Makes: A Catholic Vision of Faith, Communion, and Culture* (New York: Crossroad Publishing, 2009), 17–21.

society. They gave it dynamism not only as a republic but more importantly as a republic of Christians, who believed in popular sovereignty precisely because they *were* Christians. "The Middle Ages knew the meaning of the sovereignty of the people," Murray pointed out. "The genius of the American system lies rather in the bold answer to the urgent nineteenth-century question, 'Who are the people?' After some initial hesitation America replied forthrightly, 'Everybody, on a footing of equality.'"[8]

Americans assumed that citizens could "live a life of reason, exercise their birthright in freedom, and assume responsibility" for public affairs. Consequently, they founded a limited national government meant only to promote the conditions necessary for peace, justice, and prosperity so that the real work of mankind—the "spiritual task" of knowing, loving, and serving God—might go ahead. The primary condition was freedom. Murray acknowledged Catholic condemnations of aspects of the American political theory but argued that the condemnation applied to "the type of government based on radically rationalist principles that emerged from the French Revolution. A condemnation of the American idea is implied only because there has been an official failure to take explicit account of the fact that the American political system and its institutions are not of Revolutionary and Jacobin inspiration."[9]

Like Tocqueville, Murray wisely discerned the crucial difference between the American and French Revolutions. Unfortunately, nineteenth-century Catholic leaders, including some popes, did not always do so. Catholic social teaching as it has developed since *Rerum Novarum*, however, has done so, as succeeding chapters in this book will show.

When Americans talked about liberty, they referred to their concrete liberties first as Englishmen and then as Americans.

---

8   Murray, *We Hold These Truths*, ix, 181.
9   Murray, *We Hold These Truths*, 181–83.

These were lived and inherited freedoms, not ideological assertions realized through blood and terror. The only question was whether they were due to all men or to a select few. Thomas Jefferson indicated in the Declaration of Independence that these liberties were universal. Others thought they were a uniquely white European inheritance. Jefferson's words belong to the first category, his actions to the second. This tension between the universal and the particular, personified in Jefferson, was present at the beginning.

There are scholars who, like Murray and Chesterton, accept the existence of an American founding but disagree with them over its nature. They argue that it was a hard founding based almost entirely on Enlightenment principles as the first French Revolution was. The best current example of this is Patrick Deneen's *Why Liberalism Failed*. Deneen calls the United States "the first nation founded by the explicit embrace of liberal philosophy, whose citizenry is shaped almost entirely by its commitments and vision." He argues that the liberalism promoted by the founders "above all advances a new understanding of liberty." The old definition of liberty, rooted in Greece, Rome, and Christendom, relied on individual virtue in search of the common good. This ancient definition was thrust aside by the unholy trinity of Thomas Hobbes, Francis Bacon, and John Locke in favor of one steeped in radical self-interest and appetite. Culture contains the customs and traditions that limit individuals' appetites, so it would need to be destroyed. Even nature's limits would need to be overcome. Autonomous individuals are unlikely to love their own place, for their place might be what is stifling their autonomy. As the autonomous individual does not want to kneel before the past, neither does he want to be mindful of the future. His is an eternal present where the state guarantees fulfillment of his wildest desires, even when those desires are unnatural, unwise, or both. In the end, according to Deneen, only a strong and centralized state can make this kind of libertine life possible.[10]

This is the liberalism, says Deneen, that was "first instantiated as a political experiment by the Founders of the American liberal republic."[11] And because this liberalism was based on the false anthropology of radical human autonomy and not on the same Christian anthropology that gave birth to concepts such as liberty and virtue in the first place, the American experiment was doomed to fail. "The liberated individual" would require "the controlling state" to fulfill his passions or confirm him in his passivity, all the while chipping away at liberalism's foundations. The founders unwisely took for granted the continuation of all those things that liberalism is designed to destroy: "the health and continuity of families, schools, and communities."[12]

This might be sound *intellectual* history, and indeed Deneen is at his best in his explanation of modernity and America's liberal-conservatives and conservative-liberals. But his telling of the founding is not a fulsome and complex history of human events. As Samuel Goldman argues in his critique of *Why Liberalism Failed*, there is an ahistorical argument of inevitability when we attribute "profound social and political changes to arguments in philosophical treatises." As Goldman puts it, "It may be true that the philosophical currents that Deneen traces back to Bacon were necessary conditions for the American founding. But they were neither sufficient nor determinative." In acknowledging only these intellectual factors we risk "a kind of inverted Whig history," finding "decline and corruption where liberals expected progress." Such ahistorical analysis neglects the important ways in which the American republic was not "founded" at all and

---

[10] Patrick Deneen, *Why Liberalism Failed* (New Haven and London: Yale University Press, 2018), 5, 48–49, 72, 77, 99.

[11] Deneen, *Why Liberalism Failed*, 28, 32, 45.

[12] Deneen, *Why Liberalism Failed*, 38–42.

the ways in which its classical republicanism and diversity of Christians have shaped and continue to transform its culture. Making liberty possible, as Gleaves Whitney has noted, were moral, intellectual, political, legal, and even social limits. As long as America's Christian culture and civic republicanism tempered the individualistic and statist excesses of liberalism, it would be hard to find a place that has been friendlier to a rightly ordered liberty.[13]

This leads us to the second main school of thought we must consider when assessing the compatibility of the American experiment with CST, one that is neither as ahistorical and theory-driven as Deneen's in its condemnation of American democracy nor as committed to the idea of a hard founding as Murray's when praising the American proposition. Russell Kirk is the best example of this second school of thought, which rejects the idea of a hard American founding.

Kirk believed that the United States was exceptional and that it had a mission. This mission was no programmatic quest for a utopia based on the passing ideology of an age. Rather, it was a mission to see if a self-governed people could balance liberty with order, under law and to the maximization of justice. Justice, order, and freedom, Kirk claimed, are the "three cardinal ideas" of American civilization. Each "dominated the minds of the founders of our Republic."[14] Kirk held that America was not a new creation born of Enlightenment liberalism or rooted in any other ideology. Rather, it was the preservation of an old,

---

[13] Samuel Goldman, "The Inevitability of Liberal Failure?" *University Bookman* (January 15, 2018), www.kirkcenter.org/bookman/article /the-inevitability-of-liberal-failure; Gleaves Whitney, "Afterword," in Russell Kirk, *The American Cause* (Regnery, 1957; repr., Wilmington: Intercollegiate Studies Institute, 2002), 150–51.

[14] Russell Kirk, *The American Cause* (Regnery, 1957; repr., Wilmington: Intercollegiate Studies Institute, 2002), 50–51.

complex, long-developed civilization, rooted in London, yes, but also in the political, philosophical, and moral traditions of Athens, Jerusalem, and Rome.[15] In essence, Americans had engaged in a revolution not to promote radical ideologies or to defend universal, egalitarian claims but to preserve their traditional liberties. Good order in such a society would rely more on virtue and tradition than on state power, for Americans knew all too well how easily the power of a state or a state church could be abused.

The next step for Americans was to codify their order in a constitution to preserve and perpetuate a judicious balance between liberty and order. This included, most prominently, religious freedom. The "combination of complete toleration of opinion with no national attachment to religious principle is very rare in the world," Kirk wrote. "Most nations either recognize—formally or implicitly—a state religion, or else disavow religious truth altogether. Such a harmony between church and state is one of the principal achievements of American society."[16]

The United States was no less than a genuine development of Christian (or Western) civilization, and specifically, of English civilization. The framers combined their own lived experience as a free and religious people with English common law traditions, English constitutionalism, "and to their English legacy the founders of our Republic added Roman features."[17] The government of the City of Man would do the minimum necessary to preserve order while the City of God would be left free to transform culture and society. In such a culture, Catholics

---

[15] Kirk, *American Cause*, 51. For Kirk's fullest argument on this topic, see *Roots of American Order* (1974; rep., Wilmington: Intercollegiate Studies Institute, 2003).

[16] Kirk, *American Cause*, 38.

[17] Kirk, *American Cause*, 47–48.

no doubt could provide a Christian witness "drawing out …
the full meaning of its noblest intentions."[18]

That the authors of the *Federalist Papers* wanted to maximize
the US government's power (Alexander Hamilton) or break
down local attachments via individualism (James Madison and
Hamilton) or bar Catholics from voting and holding office (John
Jay), does not erase what happened in the ensuing decades that
began with the George Washington Administration. While
Americans did later appeal to the *Federalist Papers*, they also
associated, formed parties, divided into factions, and built
churches. That they did this to such a great degree is precisely
what Tocqueville cited as the real strength of the American
democracy and what prevented the chronic instability France
faced after its attempt at a hard, ideological, and antireligious
revolution in the name of rights so abstract that they came without duties or moral and natural limits. This penchant for small
associations and even regional ones, not to mention political
parties, only increased with time.

Is the United States a country with a creed, as Chesterton
says? Or is it something else, descended from long tradition, as
Kirk says? Could it be both: a creedal nation born during the
Enlightenment but rooted in a Christian heritage that is compatible in important ways with CST as it has developed since
Rerum Novarum? How we answer these questions leads us to
stress either the important documents of the founding period,
such as the Declaration of Independence and Constitution,
or to deemphasize these in favor of looking at how English
North America evolved into the United States of America. In
both cases, we are primed to seek out meaning in some causal
moment or original source.

In the rest of this book, I will argue that the best way to assess
the American experiment in light of CST is to take a closer look

---

[18] John Paul II, Homily at Camden Yards.

at the founding period's background and actual events. This will help us contextualize the Declaration of Independence, the Constitution, and the crucial American freedom, religious liberty. We must remain mindful that no political order is fully compatible with Catholicism or the Christian dispensation. We must do so if we are to avoid becoming ideologues and thereby weaken our use of the virtue of prudence in human affairs. The Christian faith and the gift of Catholic social teaching have a transcendent, leavening, and transformative role to play in any civilization where they are to be found.

II   Religious Liberty
in Colonial America

The question of the compatibility of the American project in liberal democracy with Catholic social teaching (CST) begins not with the story of Thomas Hobbes, John Locke, or the Enlightenment, but rather with the story of religious liberty in seventeenth- and eighteenth-century English North America. As the American revolutionaries themselves recognized, the root of all their liberties lay in liberty of conscience and religion. Before we examine the founding, then, we ought to ensure we understand the European and colonial religious milieu that existed when the thirteen colonies were founded.

The immediate historical context for the English settlements in North America was the long-lasting aftermath of the "Reformation from above," led by Henry VIII and his Protestant children, Edward and Elizabeth. The broader context is the age of persecution, violence, and state-established churches in Europe. Confessional states had an array of legal disabilities on those religions that were tolerated. Each British colonist, Catholic or not, was subject to a Protestant king or queen who was also the head of their national church, the Church of England.

In 1775 Edmund Burke coined the term *salutary neglect* to explain the explosive American response in the 1760s and 1770s to Parliamentary statutes that ran afoul of English common law, the English constitution, and long tradition.[1] The neglect of the colonies by King and Parliament had, after 160 years, produced a prosperous civilization whose people were jealous of their liberties and local government. They valued liberty because they had seen its benefits and lived free of direct English rule for several generations. When the crony capitalism of Parliament and the East India Tea Company ignored this long tradition, the Americans resisted, first in rebellion, then in revolution. This salutary neglect allowed religious diversity to flourish as well, for there existed no control from the mother country. There was not one Anglican bishop in all the Americas, and bishops in England were unsure just who had jurisdiction across the Atlantic. Meanwhile, a succession of kings dumped Quakers, Catholics, and Puritans in the Thirteen Colonies to get rid of them.

At first glance there seems to have been little liberty in a place like colonial Massachusetts. John Winthrop and the Puritans settled Massachusetts Bay in 1630 with the express religious conviction to be a "city on a hill"—a model to Europe. Worldly Europe would repent once it saw that a godly commonwealth was possible on Earth. The Church of England would also complete its purification of Catholic dogma, ecclesiology, and practice. Yet, from the start, dissenters such as Roger Williams proposed a complete separation of civil and religious authority. This proposition was a radical solution to keep the saints uncorrupted. The trial of Williams, and later of Anne Hutchinson, showed what kind of power Governor Winthrop wielded in civil and religious affairs.

Winthrop's New England was an authoritarian community by choice but also by necessity because of its isolation in the

---

[1] Edmund Burke, Speech to Parliament, 22 March 1775, in *The Works of the Right Honourable Edmund Burke*, 6 vols. (London: Henry G. Bohn, 1854–1856), 1:464–71.

North American wilderness. Success and prosperity were its biggest problem where the hopes of its founders were concerned. Prosperity attracted new settlers who disagreed with Winthrop's religious vision. It became increasingly difficult with so large and diverse a population for Winthrop and the magistrates to enforce their authority. True to puritanism, each congregation also fought to define its own orthodoxy.

In working through this difficulty, Winthrop talked about two types of liberty. "Natural liberty ... is common to man with beasts and other creatures," he said. "It is a liberty to do evil as well as to do good." This was an individual's liberty. On the other hand, "civil liberty" arises out of "politic covenants and constitutions," like the civil liberty granted by the royal charter of 1629. Winthrop argued that civil liberty was "maintained and expressed in a way of subjection to authority." He told the colonists that they must "quietly and cheerfully submit unto that authority which is set over you, in all the administration of it, for your own good."[2]

The religious historian Mark Noll argues that the Puritans despised republicanism because they tied it to Enlightenment skepticism about religion and authority. Other historians have focused their condemnation of the Puritans on their oppression of dissenters and Winthrop's strong ruling hand. In one way or the other, these historians say we ought not trace American republican ideas to the Puritans.[3]

While they certainly were not democratic, the Puritans, according to Michael Winship in *Godly Republicanism*, did hate arbitrary authority (i.e., tyranny). More importantly, they

---

[2] John Winthrop, "On Liberty," Speech before the General Court of Massachusetts, 1645, http://www.constitution.org/bcp/winthlib.htm.

[3] See Mark Noll, *America's God: From Jonathan Edwards to Abraham Lincoln* (Oxford: Oxford University Press, 2005).

governed themselves without bishops, without nobles, and without direction from the Crown or Parliament. Like Edmund Burke before him, Tocqueville saw the importance of this quite clearly. He described the Christian faith in America, due to its origins among people who "acknowledged no other religious supremacy" outside themselves, "as democratic and republican." "From the start," writes Tocqueville, "politics and religion were in agreement and they have continued to be so ever since."[4] The Puritans may have been concerned only for their own liberty, but they did a lot of thinking about the interaction of liberty, virtue, and the common good.

Along with this mixed Puritan inheritance, another major influence on the development of American liberty was William of Orange's Act of Toleration (1689). When Charles II was restored to the throne in 1660 following nearly twenty years of civil war and strife, he remained friendly to Catholicism. His brother James, heir to the throne, was Catholic. So when Charles suspended Parliamentary laws against Catholics and Puritans, Parliament passed the Test Act. The Test Act stated that only Anglicans could hold military and civil offices. Parliament then tried to pass the Exclusion Bill. This stated that no Catholic could be monarch, effectively barring the rise of James to the throne.

Charles's response in 1681 was to suspend Parliament. When he died in 1685, James II became king and imposed a new order of religious toleration on England. He violated the Test Act but there was no rebellion because of his advanced age. His only successors were two Protestant daughters, Mary and Anne.

---

[4] Tocqueville, *Democracy in America*; New York: Penguin Books, 2003), 336; Edmund Burke, Speech to Parliament, 22 March 1775, 464–71. See also Michael Winship, *Godly Republicanism: Puritans, Pilgrims, and a City on a Hill* (Cambridge: Harvard University Press, 2012).

In 1688, though, when James had a son by his second wife, Parliamentary representatives visited Mary in the Netherlands and asked her husband, William of Orange, to take the Crown by force. William raised an army, invaded England, and James and his family fled to France.

William's actions reached the colonies, extending this Protestant ascendency even to Maryland, a Catholic colony established under Charles I. In 1649 Lord Baltimore had approved the Maryland Toleration Act, the first such act in all the English colonies. The act tolerated all Trinitarian Christians while preventing public criticism of another person's religion. This toleration came to an end with the overthrow of James II. Protestant settlers formed an "Association in Arms for the Defense of the Protestant Religion," which expelled Catholic officials, outlawed Catholic education, outlawed public Mass, and taxed Catholics at double the rate of Protestants. It is worthy of note that the first real religious liberty in English North America came not in Massachusetts Bay but in the Catholic colony of Maryland.

Under William, there was more "toleration" as well, as the term was understood at the time. William's Act of Toleration called for toleration of all except non-Trinitarians and Catholics. Jews were suspect for their perceived non-Englishness as were Catholics, who were presumed to be more loyal to the pope than to the king. Only the Church of England, headed by the Dutch William, would have full political rights. This was religious liberty as the American colonists knew it: a confessional state with one established church where most but not all religions were allowed, each with varying legal restrictions as one descended down the ladder from the established church.

Winthrop's conception of civil liberty and the legacy of the Act of Toleration shaped government in America well into the eighteenth century. By the 1730s there existed several established churches, each with its own legal privileges. In the middle colonies, religious and ethnic diversity meant there was no single established church. Quaker Pennsylvania was the only colony that did not tax in the name of religion, and this made it distinctive not only in the colonies but also in Europe. In New York, in the name of liberty, each local community chose its own church and duly supported it with local taxes.

Then came the so-called Great Awakening of the 1730s and 1740s, a series of evangelical revivals so widespread that historians consider it the first real "American event." It was "American" in that it was not confined to one colony. The Great Awakening stressed that all could be saved and was characterized by simplified Protestant doctrine. Along with its emphasis on a singular conversion experience, these ideas tended to promote religious liberty because they washed over Protestant doctrinal disputes.

In terms of the story of religious freedom in America, the legacy of the Great Awakening is that it laid the groundwork for the further expansion of religious freedom. It marked a genuine development of human understanding that liberty, and religious liberty, specifically, could be a preservative and stable influence on societal order rather than a destructive one. The American colonial experience with religious liberty, imperfect though it was, had shown this to be the case. Or in the words of *Dignitatis Humanae*, "in order that relationships of peace and harmony be established and maintained within the whole of mankind, it is necessary that religious freedom be everywhere provided with an effective constitutional guarantee and that respect be shown for the high duty and right of man freely to lead his religious life in society."[5]

The Great Awakening did not end religious persecution in America any more than the First Amendment did so a few decades later. Neither could erase envy, fear, and hatred from the human heart. The Great Awakening did, however, advance

---

[5] Second Vatican Council, Declaration on Religious Liberty (*Dignitatis Humanae*), no. 15.

religious liberty by showing that persons of different religions could live peacefully in the same society. Along with the events that were to follow in the long American Revolution, the Great Awakening helps show that the United States was not founded with a creedal blueprint drawn up by Enlightenment liberals indifferent to and skeptical of religion. Rather, freedom of religion in America developed as part of a long struggle for liberty and a lived experience with its blessings. It was an imperfect inheritance, eventually protected by the Constitution and then enhanced by practice. "The American order ... was not founded upon ideology," writes Russell Kirk: "It was not manufactured; rather, it *grew*."[6]

---

6   Russell Kirk, *Roots of American Order* (1974; repr., Wilmington: Intercollegiate Studies Institute, 2003), 9.

III   Can Catholics Support the Declaration of Independence?

Thomas Jefferson's epitaph at Monticello lists his authorship of the Declaration of Independence as one of his three greatest accomplishments. Near the end of his life Jefferson described the purpose of the Declaration this way:

> Not to find out new principles, or new arguments, never before thought of, not merely to say things which had never been said before; but to place before mankind the common sense of the subject, in terms so plain and firm as to command their assent, and to justify ourselves in the independent stand we are compelled to take. Neither aiming at originality of principle or sentiment, nor yet copied from any particular and previous writing, it was intended to be an expression of the American mind, and to give to that expression the proper tone and spirit called for by the occasion.[1]

While the Declaration's philosophical claims about the nature of man, liberty, equality, and limited government found a broad consensus among the patriots, that consensus emerged amid

---

[1]   Thomas Jefferson to Henry Lee, 8 May 1825, in *Thomas Jefferson: Writings*, ed. Merrill D. Peterson (New York: Library of America, 1984), 1500–1501.

tensions over each of these things. Congress edited Jefferson's initial draft, removing those items that might shatter the growing consensus for independence, such as his condemnation of slavery. It is instructive, therefore, to situate the Declaration in time and place. Like the Constitution after it, the Declaration's final text was a compromise.

The Declaration of Independence was the fruit of organic development in the English common law tradition—wrapped in some universalist and "rights" language, to be sure, but particularist nonetheless about the "traditional liberties of Englishmen" that had been repeatedly violated. Jefferson's goal with the Declaration was not to provide a systematic treatise on government. It was to give a rationale that could convince the world that Americans were not just tax-evading smugglers but had real grievances and after much forbearance were performing their duty to throw off the yoke of British tyranny.

The cause of independence grew out of the colonial rebellion against British efforts to rule its North American colonies more directly following the end of the French and Indian War in 1763. The Writs of Assistance, Sugar Act of 1764, Stamp Act of 1765, Townshend Duties of the late 1760s, and Tea Act of 1773 each in some way ended Britain's policy of exempting the American colonies from revenue measures, demanded that all goods pass through Britain before being exported from the Empire, came with a confusing bureaucracy, and violated one or more traditional English legal rights.

Sam Adams and the Sons of Liberty protested the Tea Act with the Boston Tea Party in December 1773. Parliament responded in April 1774 by revoking the charter of Massachusetts, forbidding common law juries for some offenses, closing Boston Harbor, and confiscating private property. When the First Continental Congress met in September 1774 to address these "Intolerable Acts," it had in hand a document written by Jefferson, the "Summary View of the Rights of British America." The word *rights* appears numerous times in this document. Jefferson states that Americans are not asking for rights but for favors. They cannot ask for rights, he says, because they already possess *some* rights under God and *other* rights as Englishmen thanks to the common law tradition. He argues that Parliament has stepped on "those rights which God and the laws have given equally and independently to all." Jefferson also talks about rights "which nature has given to all men." Among these are "free trade with all parts of the world, possessed by the American colonist, as of natural right, and which no law of their own land had taken away or abridged" until Parliament "unjustly" did so.

Already we get the sense in the "Summary View" of something seen more clearly in the Declaration of Independence: Americans believed their liberty came from God and that in its proper exercise there were legitimate limits. This is solid Augustinian thinking, unsurprising from a people with an ancient Christian heritage. In the words of the *Catechism of the Catholic Church*, "The right to the exercise of freedom … must be recognized and protected by civil authority within the limits of the common good and public order."[2] Americans were not making a request for new rights abstracted from eighteenth-century philosophy. As Tocqueville later pointed out, "America was a new nation, yet people who lived there had long been accustomed to the exercise of liberty elsewhere." More importantly, in the thirteen colonies they had lived from time out of mind in a prudent balance of liberty and order.[3]

The *Oxford English Dictionary's* (*OED*) first definition of *liberty* is, "Exemption or release from captivity, bondage, or slavery." The *OED's* second definition refers to, "Exemption or freedom from arbitrary, despotic, or autocratic rule or control," while the third defines liberty as, "The condition of being able to

---

2   *Catechism of the Catholic Church*, no. 1738.

3   Tocqueville, *Democracy in America*, 148.

act in any desired way without restraint; the power to do what one likes." The first two are negative definitions, understanding human freedom only in terms of what one has been freed from. The third would be a better definition of licentiousness. What each definition has in common is that it differs so mightily with the understanding of liberty in eighteenth-century America and with the definition of freedom found in the *Catechism of the Catholic Church.*

According to the *Catechism*, "Freedom is the power, rooted in reason and will, to act or not to act, to do this or that, and so to perform deliberate actions on one's own responsibility."[4] This freedom "attains its perfection when directed toward God." Thus, the "more one does what is good, the freer one becomes. There is no true freedom except in the service of what is good and just.... Progress in virtue, knowledge of the good, and ascesis enhance the mastery of the will over its acts."[5]

Americans at the time of the founding talked more of "liberties" than liberty. In particular they talked about the "traditional liberties of Englishmen," which they had inherited. Generally, they meant an "ordered liberty," wherein a balance is struck between protecting individual freedom and promoting the common good. A negative definition of liberty, as entirely a freedom *from* something else, would not have been understandable to eighteenth-century Americans. Their liberty was not just a matter of freedom from restriction; it came with duties, too. This was the right to be free in order to do good—a very different thing from one's freedom to pursue one's own ends, no matter the consequences. This is in keeping with the patristic tradition and with St. Thomas Aquinas: Liberty is not merely choice, but must be properly ordered to the Good, not only of

---

4   *Catechism of the Catholic Church*, no. 1731.

5   *Catechism of the Catholic Church*, nos. 1733–1734.

the person but of society. True freedom is the ability to be able to do what one ought to do.

The classically educated Jefferson rejected an old Ciceronian definition of liberty as the right to do what the law allows. Instead, Jefferson argued that "rightful liberty is unobstructed action according to our will within the limits drawn around us by the equal rights of others.[6] Law, thought Jefferson, can too often be the tyrant's will. This is similar to the Catholic understanding of freedom in that every human person possesses the same dignity and freedom and must not abuse his freedom. But there is one important difference, in that the Church's gauge is not "the equal rights of others" but rather goodness and justice. "There is no true freedom except in the service of what is good and just."[7]

It is worth investigating further what Jefferson means by "rights." Are these legal rights? Self-evident ones? Universal? Particularly English? Can they be won or lost? What recourse does one have when one's liberty is violated? What is the source of these rights? Historian Stephen Conrad observes that "Jefferson's ideas about rights defy simple characterization; they cannot be aligned with any single 'tradition' whatsoever." In fact, around this same time Jefferson elsewhere wrote about everything from "the common rights of mankind" to "constitutional rights" to "the rights of the British empire in general" and the "natural and legal rights" of Americans.[8]

These strains of thinking come together in the opening lines of the Declaration of Independence. Like most Americans in the

---

6   Thomas Jefferson to Isaac H. Tiffany, 4 April 1819, https://founders .archives.gov/documents/Jefferson/98-01-02-0303.

7   *Catechism of the Catholic Church*, no. 1733.

8   Stephen A. Conrad, "Putting Rights Talk in Its Place: *The Summary View* Revisited," in *Jeffersonian Legacies*, ed. Peter S. Onuf (Charlottesville: University of Virginia Press, 1993): 254–80.

eighteenth century, Jefferson believed liberty was a divine gift, whether that divinity be the God of the Christian Bible, his own "Nature's God," or what Washington preferred to call "Divine Providence." Jefferson recognized that if the source of our liberty does not transcend the state, then it is the state's to give and to take away. Even in a republic with popular sovereignty, in the name of the majority liberty might still be unjustly curtailed. If liberty is a gift of God, we possess freedoms simply by virtue of being human, not because a state gave them to us. One did not need John Locke to see the ramifications of this: Government exists to serve the citizenry, not the other way around, for the people as people predate the apparatus of government. Likewise, liberty must transcend the individual as well. If it does not, then liberty becomes merely each person's will to power—the might of each person over the weak becomes liberty's defining attribute and only limit.

"Man," wrote St. Irenaeus, "is created with free will and is master over his own acts."[9] This message is echoed in the Declaration of Independence:

> We hold these truths to be self-evident, that all men are created equal, that they are endowed by their Creator with certain unalienable Rights, that among these are Life, Liberty and the pursuit of Happiness. —That to secure these rights, Governments are instituted among Men, deriving their just powers from the consent of the governed, —That whenever any Form of Government becomes destructive of these ends, it is the Right of the People to alter or to abolish it, and to institute new Government, laying its foundation on such principles and organizing its powers in such form, as to them shall seem most likely to effect their Safety and Happiness.

---

[9] *Catechism of the Catholic Church*, no. 1730.

Note that it is not only a right, but also a duty, to "throw off" such a government. This is not a call for anarchy but for limited government that allows individuals to pursue happiness.

This is also the natural rights language of Locke and comes straight out of the Real Whig tradition, which straddled the line between assessing government according to the organic tradition of English common law on the one hand, and, on the other, examining every form of government through reason to see if it stood up to the concept of popular sovereignty. The Whigs saw English history as a tension between Saxon traditions of liberty, self-government, and the delegation of authority on a limited basis, and Norman traditions of arbitrary monarchy and centralization. Saxons had sought to preserve the equality and freedom that all men are born with. This fact is why life, liberty, and property must not be violated: because all have an equal right to them.

The Whigs noted that if man is born with liberty, he only loses it in one of two ways: voluntarily, as in the social contract Locke talks about, or by force. This idea is important for understanding why the Declaration of Independence talks of universal natural rights at the same time it so clearly speaks about peculiar English rights. The Saxons (the English) had fought to preserve these natural rights of mankind and had never given them away. They, like the Americans, had merely consented to be ruled, but only insofar as the British government protected life, liberty, and property. This protection is the only end of government and there is no other. If it does not do this, there is a right to revolution. In the meantime, the task is balancing this right to liberty with the need for order—and doing so while mindful of equality.

What had ensured English liberties in the past was the common law, which, when violated, had resulted in petitions and declarations against the king or parliament. Among the common law matters that became salient during the American

Revolution were that defendants could not be compelled to testify; that one could not be imprisoned without a warrant and some evidence; the presumption of innocence; the right to a speedy trial; and the right to a jury trial. Even one's sovereign could not justly curtail these rights, which were later included in the United States Bill of Rights.

The Declaration's preamble is part of this English tradition of petitions and declarations even as its grievances draw from violations against common law. Many of the actual grievances against King George III had been made against past kings. Specifically, the Declaration of Independence drew heavily from the 1628 English Petition of Right against Charles I and from the 1689 Declaration of Rights against William III, which later became the English Bill of Rights. The Petition of Right singles out unconstitutional taxes (forced loans by the king, not passed by Parliament), the forced housing of soldiers, imprisonment without cause, and the use of martial law by the king. All of these are in the Declaration in one form or another.

Jefferson's goal with the Declaration was not to provide a systematic treatise on man and the state or on law and constitutionalism. It was to give a rationale to convince the world of the righteousness of the American cause. American Independence was the result of American grievances not being redressed, not the consequence, as would be the case in France in the 1790s, of kneejerk antiauthoritarianism and radical revolutionary theories contrary to the common good.

The idea of an ancient constitution in the common law tradition does not at first glance sit well with liberalism's claims of universal and natural rights. The key point to recognize, however, is that Americans saw these two streams of thinking as inseparable. Jim Stoner puts it this way: Regardless of the intentions of John Locke in his philosophy of natural right and revolution, into his "theory were integrated doctrines and practices of English common lawyers and their notion of an ancient constitution—an unwritten constitution subject to development as well as decay but ultimately aimed at protecting English liberties." The specificity in the common law and the ancient constitution "gave the abstract theory a distinctive form, while the theory made order of the mass of particulars in the extreme case, when the question of foundations was raised not just abstractly, but politically." This, then, is the process we see in the Declaration, which at first appears so Lockean and rooted in natural rights.[10]

In gauging the compatibility of Roman Catholic teaching with the American experiment in liberal democracy, this bit of history is instructive. It shows that even in revolution Americans recognized that liberty entails limits and duties. They also believed that the source of their liberty was God, transcending both the state and the individual. More importantly, Americans rested their claims in a tradition that understood constitutional rights as universal natural rights shaped over the centuries by local concerns and developed via prudence. These universal natural rights in other language form the nucleus of Catholic social teaching about the life and dignity of the human person: "Every human person, created in the image of God, has the natural right to be recognized as a free and responsible being."[11]

Americans were not ideologues seeking to make reality fit their abstract theories about the way things ought to be. Rather, most agreed with Patrick Henry that the "only sure guide for our feet is the lamp of experience." John Dickinson said something similar at the Constitutional Convention: "Experience must be

---

10 James R. Stoner, Jr., *Common Law and Liberal Theory: Coke, Hobbes, and the Origins of American Constitutionalism* (Lawrence: University of Kansas Press, 1992), 189.

11 *Catechism of the Catholic Church*, no. 1738. See also *Compendium of the Social Doctrine*, nos. 105–14.

our only guide. Reason may mislead us." And despite its rights language, Jefferson's Declaration is best understood as the fruit of reflection on this long experience and the firm belief in laws that transcend both the individual and the state. This comports with the teaching of the *Catechism of the Catholic Church*, which states, "The *right to the exercise of freedom*, especially in moral and religious matters, is an inalienable requirement of the dignity of the human person."[12]

---

[12] Patrick Henry, Speech at the Second Virginia Convention, 23 March 1775, St. John's Church, Richmond, Virginia; John Dickinson, 13 August 1787, Constitutional Convention, Madison Debates, http://avalon.law.yale.edu/18th_century/debates_813.asp; *Catechism of the Catholic Church*, no. 1738, emphasis in original.

IV Is Religious Liberty
Religious Indifferentism?

Even as the Declaration of Independence is best seen as a product of the "Spirit of 1776" and the fight for liberty, so, too, are the other important documents produced in the forge of war between 1776 and 1777: the Articles of Confederation and the Virginia Statute for Religious Freedom. Although all three were written at about the same time, the Statute took the longest to be put into effect.

The Articles, America's first constitution, were written during wartime with the recognition that, as Benjamin Franklin allegedly said, if the states did not hang together they would hang separately. Recent experience with tyranny made protecting liberty the primary concern of the Articles. Importantly, this meant state sovereignty, not individual liberties. Individual freedom was to be left to the domestic politics of each of the states in the Union. As John Adams, who had been one of the least radical of the revolutionaries, later wrote, the men of 1776 never thought of "consolidating this vast Continent under one national government" but instead erected "a Confederacy of States, each of which must have a separate government."[1]

---

[1] John Adams, 1775, in *Letters of Members of the Continental Congress*, ed. Edmund Cody Burnett (Carnegie Institution of Washington, 1921), 1:106.

In this highly decentralized Union, state sovereignty trumped concerns about individual liberty. The Articles aimed to avoid everything that had become instruments of tyranny in British hands. As a result, there was no national military, no executive branch, and no national judiciary. The states represented in the federal government had to vote unanimously for any tax because each state was "sovereign, free, and independent." The government was composed of a unicameral Congress whose members were elected by state legislatures (not "the People"). Each state had one collective vote and oversaw all national matters via select committees. This was more of an effort to preserve the sovereignty of the states than of individuals, based on the presumption that if the sovereignty of the states was preserved then individuals' liberties would be protected as well according to each state's own laws.

By 1786, the states were barely able to repay their war debt and fund their national government's operational expenses. Factionalism and regionalism prevented commercial treaties. Meanwhile, states were ceding land to Indians in order to avoid wars but when the federal government tried to cede territory to Spain, Congress rejected the treaty. For those who would soon call themselves Federalists, this was an example not so much of too much power *per se* on the part of the states, but too much power in the exact places where a concerted national effort was absolutely necessary. Critics of the Articles said that they provided no prudent balance of liberty and order. If this was subsidiarity, it was an unworkable arrangement if the newly free states wanted to prosper and defend themselves from foreign and domestic threats.

When delegates from five states in September 1786 gathered at Annapolis, Maryland, to discuss commercial issues that the Articles were unable to resolve, they did so in the wake of Shays' Rebellion in Massachusetts. As the rebellion showed, the new central government could not even keep order. Therefore, the delegates disbanded and agreed to meet again the following year in Philadelphia to address the broader problems with the Articles.

In the meantime, another debate with equally far-reaching consequences was raging, this time in Virginia. The outcome of this debate was the passage finally in 1786 of a statute Jefferson had written in 1777, soon after authoring the Declaration of Independence and while the Articles of Confederation were still being written. The Virginia Statute for Religious Freedom is much longer than the First Amendment and it contains much that is contradictory to the Catholic understanding of why religious freedom exists and of the transformative role the Christian faith must play in any society. Jefferson relegates religious truth to mere "opinion" and states, almost mockingly for a statute, "that our civil rights have no dependence on our religious opinions any more than our opinions in physics or geometry." He also condemns ecclesiastical authority as "fallible and uninspired men," an assertion that, with respect to apostolic succession and papal infallibility, Catholics must disagree with.

Yet the Statute also bans religious taxation as sinful because it taxes people to propagate opinions they do not hold. This is a right Americans do not currently have, as they are compelled to pay for government programs that are contrary to Catholic teaching. Jefferson's statute also declares, "Almighty God hath created the mind free" and that "all attempts to influence it by temporal punishments or burthens, or by civil incapacitations tend only to beget habits of hypocrisy and meanness, and therefore are a departure from the plan of the holy author of our religion, who being Lord, both of body and mind yet chose not to propagate it by coercions on either, as was in his Almighty power to do." Jefferson's statute even speaks of truth: "And finally, that Truth is great, and will prevail if left to herself, that she is the proper and sufficient antagonist to error, and has nothing to fear from the conflict, unless by human interposition disarmed of her natural weapons free argument and debate, errors ceasing to be dangerous when it is permitted freely to contradict them."

In 1786 it still made sense to a significant number of Americans that states ought to have established churches. Religious pluralism did not mean the lack of an established church or the abolition of religious taxation. If morality came from religion, then churches needed to be supported by taxes every bit as much as other entities crucial to the common good, such as police, fire departments, and schools.

Americans naturally connected their religious liberty to their political liberty and ability to live free of government coercion large and small. This does not mean that they were not nervous about suspect groups whose beliefs were thought to be antithetical to civil and religious liberty. In America, this mainly has included Catholics and Mormons, with Muslims more recently joining the list. Until the 1950s, the story of religious liberty in America was one of an overwhelmingly Protestant population figuring out how to deal with religious plurality not just among themselves but more importantly amid massive immigration by Catholics in the nineteenth and twentieth centuries.

The Catholic Church in its social doctrine has promoted religious freedom in a clear and concise way since 1966. In so doing the Church has affirmed that "religious freedom is based on the dignity of the human person and that it must be sanctioned as a civil right in the legal order of society."[2] In fact, the *Catechism of the Catholic Church* describes respecting the religious freedom of others as one's "duty" and "part of the natural right to be recognized as a free and responsible being.... The *right to the exercise of freedom*, especially in moral and reli-

---

[2]   *Compendium of the Social Doctrine*, no. 97.

gious matters, is an unalienable requirement of the dignity of the human person."[3]

The *Compendium of the Social Doctrine of the Church* is instructive here on two points. First, it repeatedly points out, the Church responds to the particular events of a given era and to "unfamiliar and unexplored problems," along with their "social, political, and cultural impact." The Church rereads the past in light of contemporary concerns. Second, it adds to its gloss on the *Catechism* that "The meaning of freedom must not be restricted, considering it from a purely individualistic perspective and reducing it to the *arbitrary and uncontrolled exercise* of one's own personal autonomy."[4]

Rerum Novarum, for example, made this clear in addressing the labor question even as it explored the social ills and errors rising from it. This development of doctrine is seen in the area of religious freedom, too, and here we turn to what became an infamous encyclical in the United States, Pope Gregory XVI's *Mirari Vos*, issued in 1832. *Mirari Vos* is an instructive example in the importance of historical context when it comes to Catholic doctrine, as well as a more specific illustration of how the Church's teaching on religious freedom developed concurrent with Americans' practice of it.

In *Mirari Vos*, Gregory condemned "Liberalism and Religious Indifferentism." He criticized those he termed the "shameless lovers of liberty" for placing freedom of speech, conscience, and the press above civil order and religious truth. Doing so, Gregory argued, "spreads ruin in sacred and civil affairs, though some repeat over and over again with the greatest impudence that some advantage accrues to religion from it." Gregory disagreed that publishing a "flock of errors" could be "suf-

---

[3] *Catechism of the Catholic Church*, no. 1738, emphasis in original.

[4] *Compendium of the Social Doctrine*, nos. 88–91, 199, emphasis in original.

ficiently compensated by the publication of some book which defends religion and truth." Indifference to mankind's highest purpose (i.e., to know God), not a rightly ordered love for truth, lay behind appeals to "liberty of conscience," according to the pope. Quoting Augustine of Hippo, he added that, "the death of the soul is worse than freedom of error."[5]

The French Revolution and its aftermath had tried through several ideological and bureaucratic means to destroy the Christian faith in France. These efforts included reordering the calendar along rationalist lines, imprisoning or killing priests and nuns, and proclaiming the worship of Equality and Reason. Revolutionaries severed connections to the papacy and attempted to make the Church an organ of the French state. Sensing that authority itself was under attack, the pope quoted St. Paul: "There is no authority except from God; what authority there is has been appointed by God. Therefore he who resists authority resists the ordinances of God; and those who resist bring on themselves condemnation."[6]

Pope Gregory was not merely theorizing nor examining Jefferson's Virginia Statute and the First Amendment. Although he based his encyclical largely on the scriptural commentaries by Thomas Aquinas, *Mirari Vos* represents Gregory's reaction to the blood and destruction wrought by revolutionaries against Catholics and the Church since 1789. When Gregory spoke of princes protecting the Church from radical zealots bent on death or plunder, he spoke in response to actual events such as the Jacobin Reign of Terror.

Whereas one can argue that in the context of European affairs Pope Gregory's critique of liberalism's dangers and consequences was legitimate, American Catholics realized that European

---

[5] Pope Gregory XVI, Encyclical Letter *Mirari Vos* (1832), nos. 14–15, http://www.papalencyclicals.net/greg16/g16mirar.htm.

[6] Pope Gregory XVI, *Mirari Vos*, no. 17.

norms did not always apply in republican America because tradition, customs, and social conditions were not the same. The United States had no national church, no monarchs, and no history of religious wars outside spillover incidents in the American colonies during the so-called "Glorious Revolution."

What, then, was behind Jefferson's thinking with respect to the Virginia Statute? Was this just a cloak for consequentialist toleration in the name of public order? Was it an indifference to truth?

Jefferson developed his belief in religious freedom over many years; it began with an impulse for toleration and a revolutionary's hatred of all coercion. But even for Jefferson, quintessential Enlightenment man that he was, it was also about the search for truth. Jefferson's strong support for religious freedom also grew out of his erroneous notion that only reason could judge belief. He did not think any human authority could judge belief, and he put the Catholic hierarchy and what he called "the bigotry of Jesuitism" in this category. He mocked what he called the "artificial scaffolding" placed by "religion builders" around the "pure doctrines of Jesus," confident that freedom and reason would lead to a "rational Christianity." In this way, he very much had the Enlightenment thinker's unwitting trust in a truncated reason that *a priori* rejected the possibility of revealed truth. In *Notes on the State of Virginia,* Jefferson wrote, "Reason and free inquiry are the only effectual agents against error. Give a loose to them and they will support the true religion by bringing every false one to their tribunal."[7] Pope Pius IX, in his 1864 *Syllabus of Errors*, specifically condemned the idea that "Human reason,

---

[7] Thomas Jefferson to Timothy Pickering, 27 February 1821; Thomas Jefferson to John Adams, 11 April 1823, in *Jefferson's Extracts from the Gospels: "The Philosophy of Jesus" and "The Life and Morals of Jesus"*, ed. Dickinson W. Adams, Ruth W. Lester, and Eugene R. Sheridan (Princeton: Princeton University Press, 1983): 403,

without any reference whatsoever to God, is the sole arbiter of truth and falsehood, and of good and evil." Jefferson easily fits under this condemnation. Yet he was open to transcendence and knew enough when he wrote the Declaration of Independence to place the source of unalienable human rights in humanity's origin in a common, transcendent Creator. In his pursuit of truth, Jefferson always remained a theist.[8]

Jefferson's ideas on tolerance and religious liberty in some ways were rooted in John Locke, whom he admired. Locke had written that no civil authority had the right to punish individuals for religious belief. But he did not really mean it, for when Locke talked about religious toleration, he meant that the Church of England should tolerate every religious community except the Roman Catholic Church, the Society of Friends, and Jews. Each of the three bore some element of non-Englishness and was therefore suspect in terms of its patriotism. Jefferson wanted to provide a corrective to Locke where religious freedom was concerned. His positive experience in Virginia with freedom and negative experience in Europe with corrupt confessional states told him this could and should be done. Put differently, Jefferson based his thinking not on liberal ideas, as such, but on the reality of his own and others' experience in America. Besides his commitment to human freedom, which made religious freedom an inalienable right, Jefferson also thought that state coercion could never be successful anyway. In that regard, he also was practical.

The linkage between civil and religious liberty in the minds of Americans did not abate in 1786. It reached a high point with the First Amendment to the Constitution that was soon to replace the Articles of Confederation. We ought not let

---

412–13; Thomas Jefferson, *Notes on the State of Virginia* (1787), Query XVII.

[8] Pope Pius IX, *Syllabus of Errors*, no. 3.

Jefferson's own religious views cloud the importance of his role in the growth of religious liberty, a "fundamental human right." Likewise, while Americans would do much that was illiberal and violent in the name of civil and religious liberty (for example, the recurrent anti-Catholic outbursts during the 1800s), it is no less true that, as Fr. Robert Sirico puts it, religious liberty is one area where we see quite clearly "the impact of the American experiment on the teaching of the universal church." This development achieved clarity in *Dignitatis Humanae*, a more lucid and thoughtful document on religious freedom than Jefferson's statute.[9]

---

[9] *Compendium of the Social Doctrine*, pt. 2, chap. 8, § 6a; Robert Sirico, *Catholicism's Developing Social Teaching: Reflections on* Rerum Novarum *and* Centesimus Annus (Grand Rapids: Acton Institute, 1992), 43.

V   Subsidiarity, the Human Person, and the United States Constitution

"Experience," wrote Alexis de Tocquevílle in *The Old Regime and the Revolution*, "teaches that the most critical moment for bad governments is the one which witnesses their first steps toward reform."[1] While Tocquevílle was referring to the last days of the *Ancien Regime* in France, his dictum also could be applied to the United States in the 1780s, when Americans established the Articles of Confederation, abrogated it after less than six years, and then wrote a second constitution. The drive to replace the Articles with a new constitution came in the wake of the Virginia disestablishment fight. In this new debate, Patrick Henry and James Madison again found themselves in opposition. Henry became a leader among the Anti-Federalists who opposed the new Constitution and James Madison would be among its greatest proponents.

In May 1787, fifty-five delegates from every state but Rhode Island met in Philadelphia. Rather than amend the Articles, they instead began to draft a new constitution, starting with the Virginia Plan, which was decidedly in favor of order through centralization. It called for proportional representation in a

---

1   Alexis de Tocqueville, *The Old Regime and the Revolution*, trans. John Bonner (New York: Harper & Brothers, 1856), https://oll. libertyfund.org/titles/2419#de-Tocqueville_1597_591.

bicameral congress and gave Congress a veto over state laws and the power to appoint the nation's president and judges. By mid-September, delegates finally reached a compromise, which among other things included equal representation for states in the upper house and proportional representation by population in the lower house. Following final approval of the Constitution on September 17, 1787, delegates presented it to the United States.

Anti-Federalists were concerned about the potential coercive powers of the new government and the corruption of virtue. Prominent Anti-Federalists included George Clinton of New York; Virginians Richard Henry Lee, George Mason, and Patrick Henry; and Luther Martin of Maryland. Yet it was the less famous Robert Yates of New York and Samuel Bryan of Pennsylvania who laid out arguments that John Jay and James Madison refuted in detail in three of the most famous *Federalist* essays: no. 2, no. 10, and no. 51.

- (Bryan) Centinel no. 1, October 1, 1787
- (Yates) Brutus no. 1, October 18, 1787
- (Jay) Federalist no. 2, October 31, 1787
- (Madison) Federalist no. 10, November 22, 1787
- (Yates) Brutus no. 6, December 27, 1787,
- (Madison) Federalist no. 51, February 6, 1788

The timeline of this rhetorical fight shows just how occasional the Federalist Papers really were, written in a back-and-forth debate often determined by what the Anti-Federalists said first.

Bryan attacked the Constitution's checks and balances, saying these would not protect liberty but only serve to obfuscate federal corruption. Bryan also argued that one representative in the House for thirty thousand inhabitants was "too few to communicate the ... local circumstances and sentiments of so extensive" a country. (Both solidarity and subsidiarity would suffer, to put the problem in Catholic terms.) Like George Mason and other Anti-Federalists, Bryan especially lamented the absence of a Bill of Rights. He feared "a permanent aristocracy" unaccountable to "the great body of the people" because it was so far removed from them.

Although Bryan claimed that the United States' size would produce tyranny while preventing Congress from understanding local needs, he still believed a decentralized republic could maintain the order needed to keep liberty secure. Yates was not as optimistic, noting that only two countries in 1787 were as large as the United States: Russia and China. Autocrats ruled both, one claiming the Mandate of Heaven and the other taking his title from Julius Caesar (i.e., *Tsar*). Historically, large territorial republics actually endangered liberty because there was no way other than coercion to balance their many regional and factional interests. "In so extensive a republic" as the United States, Yates said, "the great officers of government would soon become above the control of the people and abuse their power for the purpose of aggrandizing themselves."

Yates singled out Congress's taxation power and the Supreme Court as the most likely avenues to despotism. Since Congress could approve taxes to "provide for the common safety, and the general welfare," taxation would be unlimited. "The government," warned Yates, "would always say their measures were designed and calculated to promote the public good; there being no judge between them and the people, the rulers themselves must, and would always, judge for themselves." Meanwhile, the Supreme Court, as constructed, would not be guided at all by natural law, precedent, or any other law, just by its own whims and whatever precedents it might set.

Federalists posed counterarguments to all these accusations. They claimed the "general welfare" clause actually limited the government's range of power. Where Anti-Federalists saw a future consolidated nation-state inherent in the Constitution,

Federalists beheld a firm grounding for a lasting federal union that balanced liberty with order. This is exactly what Madison argued in Federalist no. 10 and no. 51, in which he flipped on its head the maxim that factionalism in large republics breeds disorder, followed by either tyranny or disunion. In a nod to what G. K. Chesterton later called that most provable Christian dogma, original sin, Madison acknowledged that the "causes of faction are sown in the nature of man." Since the causes of faction cannot be removed, Madison noted realistically, to be free Americans required a polity founded on the principle of ordered liberty to control its effects.

Federalists claimed the Constitution would restrain factionalism far better than had the Articles. How? Certainly not through coercion, Madison said. Nor would it depend on enlightened aristocrats, for "enlightened statesmen will not always be at the helm." Madison acknowledged that "liberty is to faction as air is to fire," but argued that the country's diversity would prevent any majority from stepping on minority rights even as it mitigated congressional attempts to pass unwise laws. In the same way that a representative government was superior to a purely democratic one because of its greater ability to field temperate, prudent leaders, so would a large republic be superior to a small one. "We behold a republican remedy for the diseases most incident to republican government," wrote Madison in Federalist no. 10. The difficulty for Madison was that his acknowledgement of American plurality conceivably could feed Anti-Federalist fears about heterogeneous republics.

One could argue that America indeed was *founded* in that certain of the Federalist Papers served as a blueprint for the American republic. It is certainly true that later Americans drew from these in the way a communist ideologue might draw from Marxist writings when designing a government. But the story of the Federalist debate reveals these to have been occasional essays, written to convince New Yorkers (and, admittedly, others) to vote to ratify the Constitution. Patrick Deneen argues that "Publius clearly believes and intends that better administration at the federal level will lead to the displacement of local loyalties and engagement." The reality is that "Publius" was three people, each trying to persuade his countrymen to approve the Constitution and doing so often with contradictory arguments. Jay writes reassuringly in Federalist no. 2 that "Providence has been pleased to give this one connected country to one united people—a people descended from the same ancestors, speaking the same language, professing the same religion, attached to the same principles of government, very similar in their manners and customs" even as Madison two months later contradicts him in Federalist no. 10 to argue that diversity is a great thing but not to worry, because faction will balance faction.[2]

The Constitution won ratification on June 21, 1788, mainly because of promises to Anti-Federalists that a Bill of Rights would be added as soon as possible. Another comforting thought was that George Washington, who had proven trustworthy with power, would be the first president. A broad cross section of American society supported the Federalists, because they knew that the Confederation structure was bad for trade and commerce and that the Constitution would be a vast improvement in that regard. Marxist historians have had a tough time figuring out why artisans and tradesmen—men of lower rank than the lawyers and wealthy elites—would support the Constitution, but that is only because they see the world through the lens of rich versus poor and oppressor versus oppressed. They do not see it, as the Church does and as most Americans did in 1788, in light of the desire to excel and to prosper, and the drive to create.

---

2   Deneen, *Why Liberalism Failed*, 161–74.

All of these are rooted in what the human person is and are not particularly liberal, bourgeois, or radically individualistic.[3]

Important for the course of American history, Anti-Federalists yielded to the will of the state conventions and acquiesced to the new order. There would be no violent counterrevolution, only a working out of Anti-Federalist principles under the new national government. As Patrick Henry told James Monroe in 1791, "It is natural to care for the crazy machine."[4] This is why Tocqueville *correctly* marks the "end of the American Revolution" with the advent in 1789 of the new government, presided over by George Washington under the Constitution.

Catholic Social Teaching and the American Constitution

Having now taken into account both sides in the ratification debate, it remains to determine the compatibility of CST with these constitutional principles. Because these arguments tell us much about American culture, they also tell us about religion, which is the root of culture. The key to understanding how most Americans viewed themselves and the human person in the 1780s is not to be found in the Enlightenment but rather in biblical wisdom. After all, the Bible was the most quoted source at the Constitutional Convention. (Montesquieu was second, and Locke was far down the list.) Nevertheless, whereas the Declaration of Independence invoked God and the Articles mentioned "the Great Governor of the World," the Constitution was silent on religion.

---

[3] *Catechism of the Catholic Church*, no. 1730; *Compendium of the Social Doctrine*, nos. 199–200.

[4] Patrick Henry to James Monroe, 24 January 1791, in *The Papers of James Monroe*, ed. Daniel Preston (Westport: Greenwood Press, 2006), 2:493.

One great critic of the absence of God and religious tests from the Constitution was Luther Martin of Maryland, who argued that the United States was "a Christian country" and therefore ought to distinguish in law between Christians and "infidelity or paganism." Many state constitutions did so. To Martin, the US Constitution represented the worst of secular Enlightenment thinking. He argued that "a belief in the existence of a deity" and in heaven and hell "would be some security for the good conduct of our rulers."[5] Other Anti-Federalists predicted, correctly, that the Constitution would become a much-abused instrument in the hands of those who wished to build a muscular, far-reaching government. They also foresaw that the judiciary might endanger liberty more than a quasi-monarchical president.

In *God of Liberty*, Thomas Kidd refutes the Anti-Federalist claim that the Constitution represented a secular triumph. "The framers," Kidd writes, "intended to create neither a specifically Christian government nor a 'godless Constitution.' Instead, led by James Madison, they established a new government committed to maintaining public virtue." According to Kidd, evangelical Christians and their more liberal counterparts agreed with deists and skeptics that a national church would "breed spiritual coercion and hypocrisy" while provoking "paralyzing sectarian arguments." It was the *absence* of a national church, therefore, along with a diffusion of power in the new government, that would encourage virtue and the "standard of rectitude" Martin wanted. The Constitution had "structures to prevent vice and to promote morality in the public sphere and in the actions of government itself." George Washington had posed the best formulation, in which the new government would "encourage moral public behavior" but not opine on specific theological

---

5   Quoted in Thomas S. Kidd, *God of Liberty: A Religious History of the American Revolution* (New York: Basic Books, 2010), 214.

matters, while "the clergy would steward the spiritual lives of Americans."[6] Religious liberty would promote virtue, not undermine it.

The Federalists correctly criticized the Confederation for being unable to provide the minimum order needed so that Americans could flourish as a free people. That minimum order is what the Augustinian City of Man demands. The Federalists' arguments show they understood better than Anti-Federalists how a well-ordered liberty could promote the Christian faith and maintain virtue. Had the Anti-Federalists defeated the Constitution, the Union would have soon split into multiple confederations or divided into highly separate states. The consequences for liberty under these scenarios would have been worse than the most dismal Anti-Federalist prediction about life under the Constitution. Certainly, it is difficult to see how slavery might have begun its road to extinction without the new constitutional order and its implication, in the outlawing of the international slave trade, that there was something intrinsically wrong with slavery. Slavery ultimately ended in the United States due to Christian arguments that it is an intrinsic evil, not due to constitutional arguments and Lockean rights language. This was likewise the case with the Civil Rights Movement of the 1950s and 1960s, which is why Martin Luther King, Jr., quoted St. Augustine and St. Thomas Aquinas and not Locke when he was in the Birmingham jail for intentionally breaking segregation laws.[7]

---

[6] Kidd, *God of Liberty*, 214–17.

[7] King wrote, "I would agree with St. Augustine that 'an unjust law is no law at all.' Now, what is the difference between the two? ... A just law is a man-made code that squares with the moral law or the law of God. An unjust law is a code that is out of harmony with the moral law. To put it in the terms of St. Thomas Aquinas: An unjust law is a human law that is not rooted in eternal law and natural law."

The Anti-Federalists as well as the Federalists recognized that no governmental formula could, of itself, maintain a polity in which liberty and justice would be secure. This is the key point for any Catholic to recognize before prudently considering the real-world alternatives to the American Experiment in democracy.

Federalists, like their opponents, recognized the transcendence of truth and justice, as well as the need to inculcate virtue in a free society. Both sides understood that all just laws found their ultimate source in a transcendent morality. Each acknowledged virtue as a precondition for republican government. In 1776, John Adams asked, "If there is a form of government, then, whose principle and foundation is virtue, will not every sober man acknowledge it better calculated to promote the general happiness than any other form"? Still, between Federalists and Anti-Federalists, the Federalists were less likely to expect virtue. "The few … who act upon principles of disinterestedness," wrote Washington, "are, comparatively speaking, no more than a drop in the Ocean."[8] A Constitution, prudently drawing on Enlightenment liberalism but deeply rooted in Americans' own experience as a free Christian people, would help bridge the gaps. As Adams put it, "it will be safest to proceed in all

---

Martin Luther King, Jr., "Letter from a Birmingham Jail" (16 April 1963), African Studies Center, University of Pennsylvania, https://www.africa.upenn.edu/Articles_Gen/Letter_Birmingham.html.

[8] George Washington to John Hancock, 25 September 1776, *The Papers of George Washington*, ed. Philander D. Chase and Frank E. Grizzard, Jr., Revolutionary War Series (Charlottesville: University Press of Virginia, 1994), 6:393–401. See also Jonathan W. Pidluzny and Murray S. Y. Bessette, "Avarice and Ambition in America: The Founders' Debate on the Political Place of the Selfish Passions in the Constitutional Order of the United States," *Journal of Markets & Morality* 22, no. 1 (Spring 2019): 117–46.

established modes, to which the people have been familiarized by habit."[9]

Prudence being the key here, there is little in the order codified in the Constitution that is intrinsically opposed to CST. Were the Constitution not a compromise made by people with a Christian worldview recognizing the importance of virtue but rather an ideological blueprint based on a faulty anthropology of radical individual autonomy, this would not be the case. A country based on a creed can have a faulty creed capable of bringing down the whole machine if the creed is not in accord with human nature. Communism is the most obvious example, which is why state socialism remains the only system condemned by the magisterial teaching of the Catholic Church.[10] A country speaking in creedal terms and the classical vocabulary of virtue, but rooted in its own long experience with liberty, can make do with an imperfect but "best-possible" polity. This is especially true if it allows religious freedom and respects the life and dignity of the human person, honoring his right to political and social participation in consequence of the principle of subsidiarity.

The Anti-Federalists, though perceptive when identifying problems, tended to permit the perfect to be the enemy of the good. In this they have something in common with contemporary Catholic critics of American democracy. There was no remarkable penchant in the Constitution for disorder or illiberality but there was much to ward against these tendencies. The Federalists realized this; the Anti-Federalists did not. Yet to understand the degree to which the American

---

[9] John Adams, "Thoughts on Government," 1776, in *The Portable John Adams*, ed. John Patrick Diggins (New York: Penguin Books, 2004), 234–35; Washington to Hancock, 25 September 1776, 393–401.

[10] See *Compendium of the Social Doctrine*, no. 89.

founders understood the balance between liberty and order necessary for a free people, one must not neglect the Anti-Federalists. Subsidiarity had no role in the Virginia Plan, and the Constitution as written had no guarantee for religious liberty. Anti-Federalists were responsible for modifying what would have been a highly centralized government from the very beginning had the Virginia Plan succeeded *in toto* and had Anti-Federalists such as George Mason failed to secure a Bill of Rights. The first item in that Bill of Rights—the First Amendment, to which we now turn—would make explicit the role of religious liberty in the American order.

VI The "Most Cherished of American Freedoms"

With the ratification of the US Constitution in 1788, the long American Revolution came to an end. Americans quickly amended the Constitution ten times. The first of these amendments, in part, reads, "Congress shall make no law respecting an establishment of religion, or prohibiting the free exercise thereof." Thus, as the first clause of the First Amendment to the Constitution, Americans added what Pope Benedict XVI rightly called the "most cherished of American freedoms"—religious freedom—or as the American bishops put it in 2012, "our first, most cherished liberty."[1]

One common Anti-Federalist critique of the Constitution was that it lacked an explicit guarantee that the new central government would not establish one church. Madison feared that a Bill of Rights could unintentionally limit liberties and

---

1   Pope Benedict XVI, Address to the Bishops of the United States of America on Their *"Ad Limina"* Visit, 19 January 2012, http://w2.vatican. va/content/benedict-xvi/en/speeches/2012/january/documents/hf _ben-xvi_spe_20120119_bishops-usa.html; United States Conference of Catholic Bishops Ad Hoc Committee on Religious Liberty, "Our First, Most Cherished Liberty: A Statement on Religious Liberty," 2012, http://www.usccb.org /issues-and-action/religious-librty/our-first-most-cherished-liberty .cfm.

even give the central government power to restrict the domestic practices of the states, but he relented and drew up the Bill of Rights based on over one hundred proposed amendments. The most common proposal was to protect conscientious objectors from bearing arms, usually permitting them to pay another to serve in the militia in their stead. Religious freedom did not mean only freedom to worship nor did duty to the state necessarily imply one could be conscripted and made to fight on behalf of it. As Lord Acton later put it, "Conscription is not tolerated by a people that understands and loves freedom." "Freedom," according to CST, "must also be expressed as the capacity to refuse what is morally negative, in whatever guise it may be presented."[2]

This was a view shared by many Americans, and they wanted protection against being forced to bear arms against their conscience as one aspect of any religious liberty amendment. They were not to get it explicitly in the Constitution but they were to get it in law, to some degree, over the next two centuries. Conscription, on the other hand, was later upheld by the US Supreme Court in 1918, in spite of the Thirteenth Amendment forbidding "involuntary servitude."[3] The American record is mixed when it comes to respecting religious freedom where military service is concerned, for it has been easier for the wealthy to buy their way out of service (beginning with the first draft under Abraham Lincoln during the Civil War) than for the pacifist to argue his way out of it.

---

[2] Lord Acton to Richard Simpson, 9 July 1860, in *The Correspondence of Lord Acton and Richard Simpson*, 3 vols., ed. Joseph L. Altholz, Damian McElrath, and James C. Holland (London: Cambridge University Press, 1978), 2:77–79; *Compendium of the Social Doctrine*, no. 200.

[3] Arver v. United States (1918).

The First Amendment was added to the Constitution in 1791. For the next century and a half, the story of religious liberty in American was one of an overwhelmingly Protestant population figuring out how to deal with religious plurality not just among themselves but more importantly amid massive immigration by Catholics in the nineteenth and early twentieth centuries. This sentiment produced the Native American Party of the 1840s and its better-known counterpart, the Know Nothings of the 1850s. It underlay deadly riots and arson attacks against Catholics in 1834 and 1844. This anti-Catholicism was deeply connected to Manifest Destiny sentiment, Anglo-Saxonism, and the Mexican-American War of 1846–1848. It also played a significant role in the presidential campaigns of 1884, 1928, and 1960. Catholics, to say the least, had an uphill battle in the United States when addressing the interplay between their faith and the burgeoning American democracy.[4]

In this effort, they had Alexis de Tocqueville on their side. Tocqueville, a Catholic, noted that Catholics in America were fervent believers and practitioners of their religion at the same time that they were "the most republican and democratic class." He thought that "it would be wrong to see the Catholic religion as a natural opponent of democracy." It was instead "one of the most supportive of the equality of social conditions.… It makes no compromise with anyone and applies the same standard to each person; it likes to blend all social classes at the foot of the same altar." Catholicism might look like monarchy, said Tocqueville, but remove "the prince and the conditions are more equal than in republics." Once the priests are not part of government, they and their flock are the most likely to carry

---

[4] John C. Pinheiro, *Missionaries of Republicanism: A Religious History of the Mexican-American War* (Oxford: Oxford University Press, 2014), 17–43, 65.

their beliefs into politics. Catholics are, in short, "the most obedient believers and the most independent citizens."[5]

The most important thinker in the nineteenth century when it came to Catholicism in America, however, was not Tocqueville but the convert and philosopher, Orestes Brownson. Sometimes impugned as a "religious weather vane," the New England native underwent an Augustine-like journey through many religious permutations until finally joining the Catholic Church in 1844. Brownson gave an argument so forceful in its claims about the compatibility of the American experiment with Catholic teaching that he argued Catholics would make better American democrats than their fellow Protestant citizens. This was because Catholics engaged in freedom in truth and did not, as he claimed Protestants did, partake of the "modern spirit" that "asserts the universal and absolute supremacy of man, and his unrestricted right to subject religion, morals, and politics to his own will, passion, or caprice." Democracy was only possible among a population that recognized higher authority "not as the antagonist of liberty, but as its vindicator."[6]

Of religious liberty, Brownson argued "that the American understanding of religious liberty was not at all what European radicals understood by the term." What separation of church and state meant in the United States was that the government "had a constitutional responsibility to protect the freedom of the church and the freedom of individual conscience—that

---

5   Tocqueville, *Democracy in America*, 336–38.

6   Orestes Brownson, quoted in Russell Kirk, *The Conservative Mind: From Burke to Eliot* (1953; reprint, Washington, DC: Regnery Publishing, 2001), 247. For an excellent essay on Brownson's view of the American project of balancing liberty with law, under authority and in truth, see Russell Kirk, "Orestes Brownson and the Just Society," in *The Essential Russell Kirk: Selected Essays*, ed. George A. Panichas (Wilmington, DE: ISI Books, 2007), 492–501.

was its sole responsibility to the church." The Constitution also "recognized a higher law than that of positive law and thereby protected everything that the *Syllabus* feared from a radical European concept of separation."[7] Consequently, Brownson spent much of the 1860s trying to convince Catholics that Pius IX's *Syllabus* condemned a species of liberty that had everything to do with Europe and little or nothing to do with the United States.

Similarly, when fights between Protestants and Catholics over Bible reading and prayer in public schools erupted, Brownson found himself in opposition to many Catholics and their bishops. Catholics wanted to remove Bible reading and all religious instruction from public schools on the grounds that Protestant Bibles were used and the instruction also was Protestant. Brownson's opinion was that at least the Protestants recognized "that religion could not legitimately be divorced from education." He feared the ultimate secularization of public schools as the greater evil.[8]

Beginning in the 1960s, the threat to religious liberty, and in particular to Catholic religious freedom, began to come not from evangelical Protestants and nativists but from radically secular ideologues who despised all Christians. The US government, like most Americans, had come to view secularism not as an ideology steeped in its own absolute claims but rather as a neutral stance toward reality. Thus, the government now often enforces secularism in ways that the First Amendment would prevent if Americans understood secularism as the totalizing ideology that it is. In other words, contrary to the Establishment Clause, we do have an established church in this country, but it is not really a church; it is an anti-Church, claiming neutrality but

---

7   Patrick W. Carey, *Orestes Brownson: American Religious Weathervane* (Grand Rapids: Eerdmans, 2004), 302–3.

8   Carey, *Orestes Brownson*, 365.

being decidedly unneutral even when it comes to facing historical and natural realities such as marriage and human nature.

In *Centesimus Annus*, John Paul responded to the argument that a skeptical secularism ought to be the default approach by government in a democracy, that those who embrace and adhere to the truth are "unreliable from a democratic point of view, since they do not accept that truth is determined by the majority, or that it is subject to variation according to different political trends." To the contrary, John Paul observed, "if there is no ultimate truth to guide and direct political activity, then ideas and convictions can easily be manipulated for reasons of power. As history demonstrates, a democracy without values easily turns into open or thinly disguised totalitarianism."[9]

Contemporary secularist ideologues, claiming progress, believe something very similar to those in the American past who wanted to weaken the role of religion in public life and reduce religious liberty to freedom of worship. In effect, their progress would be regress, a return to the toleration of some sects over others as a bid to keep social harmony by allowing those affected most to worship in private. Yet these new ideologues want to go further and curtail all religious freedom in the name of a proliferating array of individual and group rights. In our day secular humanists believe that the default position is theirs and that secular humanism is neutral, not realizing that secular humanism, as well as its militantly atheist offshoots, claims an orthodoxy all its own. It is a substitute for religion, not the absence of a worldview. And it bears little resemblance to the ways in which the founders imagined the interaction of religion and politics or of the United States government and the individual. The militant variety of secular humanism, unlike even Jefferson's "wall of separation" ideal, wants to scrub the public square free of all vestiges of religion, not understanding

---

[9] John Paul II, *Centesimus Annus*, no. 46.

the connection between religion and culture. (Or, perhaps the militants understand it all too well.)

The addition of the Establishment and Religious Freedom Clauses to the Constitution was a key moment in world history. This acknowledgement of a fundamental right to religious liberty predated *Dignitatis Humanae* by nearly two centuries. Definition of it in America evolved as time wore on, until the mid-twentieth century when secularists defined religious freedom as a naked public square and actually instituted in a clandestine way religious tests for office in spite of the Constitution. These tests include the use of issues related to abortion, sexuality, and marriage to discern whether one is suitable for high office. By the twenty-first century, outright attack on religious institutions has come through measures such as the Barack Obama Administration's Health and Human Services mandate for coverage of artificial contraception and state laws regulating the adoption of children.

This context is important, especially in the face of arguments that religious liberty was always doomed to failure in America once its founding liberal ideas finally atomized people while entrusting the government with plebiscitary or judicial power over the truth. In reality, recent attacks on religious liberty in America—attempts to drive a variety of Christian religious institutions out of fields intrinsic to the Christian faith, such as education, adoption assistance, and medical practice—are nothing new. They are but part of what Thomas Jefferson in the Declaration of Independence called a "Long train of abuses and usurpations" on the part of local, state, and federal governments in American history.

Indeed, they predate American history. In the era of confessional states following the Reformations of the sixteenth century, most Catholics and Protestants could agree that religious freedom was not a sought-after commodity but rather a danger to the body politic. When the Second Vatican Council proclaimed religious liberty to be a civil right because it was an inalienable human right, it did so nearly two hundred years after the passage of the First Amendment. It did so on the basis that this was in accord with the dignity of the human person as a being "endowed with reason and free will and therefore privileged to bear personal responsibility" and a "moral obligation to seek the truth, especially religious truth."[10]

Even with the First Amendment, religious freedom in America has always been a work in progress. It has required, like the protection of all liberties, the constant vigilance of the citizenry. There never was a golden era in the American past where religious liberty was not under some kind of threat from individuals, from interest groups, from government, or, sadly and often enough, from Christians themselves. Rarely has democracy been the cause. Rather, the cause has been fear and hatred, and the sins that lead to and from them. In the 1800s many Americans sincerely believed that limiting the freedom of Catholics actually *ensured* religious and civil liberties.[11]

Despite this recurrent anti-Catholicism, the Archbishop of Baltimore, James Cardinal Gibbons, while in Rome in 1887, could praise the United States as "a country where the civil government holds over us the aegis of its protection without interfering in the legitimate exercise of our sublime mission as ministers of the Gospel of Jesus Christ." In his opinion, the United States had managed to balance liberty and order, embarking on an experiment in self-government that offered "authority without despotism" and "liberty without license." This was essentially the argument of Orestes Brownson. That Catholics were thriving in the United States Gibbons attributed "in no small degree to the civil liberty we enjoy in our enlightened republic." He could say these things at a time when the

---

[10] *Dignitatis Humanae*, no. 3.

[11] Pinheiro, *Missionaries of Republicanism*, 15–35.

American bishops had recently called on every Catholic parish in the country to have a school, due to the overtly Protestant curriculum and prayers in so many American public schools. Even in the midst of an anti-Catholic culture, Gibbons insisted, the American system preserved space for Catholic flourishing.[12]

The dignity of the human person requires freedom. It also requires truth. "The *right to the exercise of freedom*," says the *Catechism of the Catholic Church*, "especially in moral and religious matters, is an inalienable requirement of the dignity of the human person."[13] As John Paul notes in *Centesimus Annus*, "obedience to the truth" is directly related to "the duty to respect the rights of others."[14] Orestes Brownson formulated the American approach this way:

> The religious mission of the United States is not then to establish a church by external law, or to protect her by legal disabilities ... but to maintain catholic freedom, neither absorbing the state in the church nor the church in the state, but leaving each to move freely, according to its own nature, in the sphere assigned it in the eternal order of things ... conforming both to the real or divine order, which is supreme and immutable.

Practically speaking, this meant that "Error has no rights but the man who errs has equal rights with him who errs not."[15]

---

12 Cardinal James Gibbons, Address upon taking possession of Santa Maria in Trastevere, March 25, 1887; quoted in USCCB Ad Hoc Committee on Religious Liberty, "Our First, Most Cherished Liberty," 1.

13 *Catechism of the Catholic Church*, no. 1738, emphasis in original.

14 John Paul II, *Centesimus Annus*, no. 17.

15 Orestes Brownson, *The American Republic*, in *The Works of Orestes A. Brownson* 20 vols. (Detroit: H. F. Brownson, Publisher, 1905), 18:217; Brownson quoted in Carey, *Orestes A. Brownson*, 255.

VII Virtue and Liberty
during the Washington
Administration

To round out our historical survey of the American founding in light of Catholic social teaching, we turn now to a brief look at the formative presidency of George Washington. Washington was not known for his deep philosophical ideas but what he bequeathed to the country was a legacy of prudential and temperate leadership. It is in Washington's leadership that we see most prominently the compatibility of CST principles with the American experiment, because in Washington's virtuous character we see prominently displayed the confluence of the Western moral and intellectual heritage in the constitutional order of the United States.

For our purposes both democracy and republican government fit well under the broader category of "liberal democracy"—a state overtly rooted in popular sovereignty but with a variety of safeguards, including the kind of multistage elections built into a constitutional republic such as the United States. Such a government is one wherein decisions are based to one degree or another on citizens' participation. Participation is a direct outgrowth of the principle of subsidiarity. Knowing this makes the early republican period of the 1790s an even more important lens through which to assess the American experiment in light of CST and to evaluate the argument that Catholicism is inimical to American liberal democracy because the American cause of ordered liberty was doomed inevitably to sink into a frenzied passion for radical autonomy.

In his speech to Congress on resigning from the Continental Army in 1783, Washington closed by "commending the Interests of our dearest Country to the protection of Almighty God." For Washington, who spoke often of Providence or the Divine Architect but rarely of God and never of Jesus Christ, this was an unusual but pointed choice of words. His other, more famous retirement announcement, the Farewell Address of 1796, would make the same point: Without religion a republic is doomed to decline rapidly. The Constitution and prescriptive laws can only do so much to guard against the dark but ineradicable aspects of human nature. If Americans really are to establish justice and insure domestic tranquility, "religion and morality are indispensable." Morality issues from religion, not the other way around. Washington condemned abstract theorizing about whether "morality can be maintained without religion." "Reason and experience," he said, "both forbid us to expect that national morality can prevail in exclusion of religious principle."

This need for "virtue" and "morality," that is, for *piety*, applies equally to the governors as to the governed. Indeed, piety "is a necessary spring of popular government." Washington operated with these principles in mind, seeking to avoid having his administration given over either to Hamilton's commercialism or Jefferson's agrarianism.

While the Republican and Federalist parties initially took shape around the Hamiltonian and Jeffersonian ideologies, they came firmly together in response to European events when the French Revolution broke out in 1789. Most Americans at first welcomed the news of the revolution. But it quickly turned more radical, and more against religion and common sense. Following the abolition of the monarchy in 1792, the republic's first constitution failed. This was followed by massacres. In January 1793 revolutionaries murdered the king and queen. Then in February they declared war on Great Britain, the Netherlands, Austria, and Spain. In 1794, Robespierre and the Jacobins unleashed their Reign of Terror. Robespierre described Jacobin goals this way: "If virtue be the spring of a popular government in times of peace, the spring of that government during a revolution is virtue combined with terror; virtue, without which terror is destructive; terror, without which virtue is impotent. Terror is only justice prompt, severe, and inflexible—it is then an emanation of virtue."[1]

This is what a truly ideological revolution looks like. It lacks both key requirements of authentic democracy: rule of law and a correct anthropology.[2] Indeed, it was the French Revolution that gave the term *ideology* to the world. And reading Robespierre is nearly sufficient explanation all by itself when it comes to contextualizing nineteenth-century papal denunciations of liberalism. The bloodletting, diabolism, and destruction wrought in the name of liberty in Europe came in successive revolutions after 1789, most notably but not limited to 1848.

But in 1789 most Americans heard the word *liberty* and thought more of *France* (their recent ally) than *Revolutionary France*—the France that then was being brought into being through blood and terror. Americans were reflexively sympathetic to the French and antagonistic toward Great Britain.

Washington asked his cabinet to deliberate on the matter. In discussions, Hamilton favored neutrality and Jefferson did not. Jefferson claimed this so-called neutrality was not neutral at all, because it would help Britain more than France due to the former's superior navy. This was true. But Jefferson was a fan of the revolution and wanted a pro-French policy. In 1793

1 Maximilien Robespierre, *Report upon the Principles of Political Morality which Are to Form the Basis of the Administration of the Interior Concerns of the Republic* (Philadelphia, 1794).

2 John Paul II, *Centesimus Annus*, no. 46.

Jefferson was still naive, swayed by his rosy view of human nature and his hopes for liberty in France. He did not pause to wonder whether the allegedly virtuous outburst of liberty in France might result in a disaster, like the 1794 Reign of Terror.[3]

By contrast, Hamilton was skeptical. The French Revolution really was the test case for radical democracy in his opinion and was failing the test miserably. But Hamilton was not innocent of ideological motives either. He realized, as did Jefferson, that war with Great Britain would undermine his financial system.

This major test of Washington's leadership held the potential for involving the fragile new United States in a ruinous war that could destroy the Union. Washington, prudent as ever, knew what some of our contemporaries have forgotten: "It is a maxim founded on the universal experience of mankind … that no nation is to be trusted farther than it is bound by its interest."[4] Washington thought the United States' future would

---

[3] In 1793 Jefferson wrote the following, referring to the Jacobins' execution without trial of guilty as well as a small number of innocents:

> I considered that sect as the same with the Republican patriots.… But time and truth will rescue and embalm their memories, while their posterity will be enjoying that very liberty for which they would never have hesitated to offer up their lives. The liberty of the whole earth was depending on the issue of the contest, and was ever such a prize won with so little innocent blood? My own affections have been deeply wounded by some of the martyrs to this cause, but rather than it should have failed, I would have seen half the earth desolated.

Thomas Jefferson to William Short, 3 January 1793, https://founders.archives.gov/documents/Jefferson/01-25-02-0016.

[4] George Washington to Henry Laurens, 14 November 1778, in *The Writings of George Washington*, 39 vols., ed. John C. Fitzpatrick (Washington, DC: U.S. Government Printing Office, 1931–1934), 13:254–57.

not be determined by European affairs. American security and prosperity depended only on whether it enjoyed the time and safety to develop economically and commercially, meanwhile cementing Americans' fondness for the Union. Americans were not ideologues and only experience could teach them the value of the Union.

The *Catechism of the Catholic Church* defines fortitude as "the moral virtue that ensures firmness in difficulties and constancy in the pursuit of the good."[5] Washington's practice of fortitude can best be understood according to St. Augustine's meaning: love bearing all for the sake of the object loved. In this case and in strictly political terms, for Washington this object was the Union. This is order leading to liberty. The Union, therefore, "ought to be considered as a main prop of your liberty, and that the love of the one ought to endear to you the preservation of the other."[6]

In the face of public opinion to the contrary, Washington declared the United States to be neutral. He did so while Congress, dominated by Republicans, was out of session. This was prudence, or "practical reason," to be sure, but it was also good politics in 1793.[7] Republicans accused Washington of being dictatorial, hostile to France, and under Hamilton's control. Meanwhile, France's new ambassador, Edmond Genet, tried to spark a war in the West between the United States and Spain and helped to launch French privateers from Charleston to attack British ships in American waters.

In 1794 the British responded by seizing American ships. To head off this conflict, Washington sent John Jay to Britain, where he secured a treaty. It was deeply unpopular but pre-

---

[5] *Catechism of the Catholic Church*, no. 1808.

[6] George Washington, Farewell Address, 19 September 1796, http:// gwpapers.virginia.edu/documents_gw/farewell/transcript.html.

[7] *Catechism of the Catholic Church*, no. 1806.

vented war. Like neutrality, Washington saw the Jay Treaty as the only prudent course of action for a young, fragile country. In his Farewell Address he defended these actions. This is the context for Washington advising Americans to deal honestly and "cultivate peace" with all nations. To Republicans, this meant peace toward Great Britain. But unmistakably this also was a message to those Federalists who wished to wage war on France. "Religion and morality enjoin this conduct; and can it be, that good policy does not equally enjoin it?" Here are echoes of Cicero and the Stoic idea that acting virtuously can never be disadvantageous. Good policy ought to flow from morality and virtue, which find their source in religion. "The permanent felicity of a nation," Washington claims, "is connected by Providence with its virtue."[8]

Washington was aware of the interconnectedness among religion, virtue, liberty, and piety. He was a nonideological man whose actions bespoke of the larger Christian and classical heritage. He sought to practice the classical and Christian virtues, even if he reputedly could not bring himself to recite the Creed. His actions as president prove the indispensability not so much of Washington himself but of virtue and Christian principles in the maintenance of the American republic.

One great benefit of an historical rather than purely theoretical approach is that it enables us to see how men and women transcend their theories and their own era's rhetoric, sometimes in spite of themselves. The historical approach also helps us recognize that men change their minds, even those we fit with labels such as "founders." The founders' ideas, like everyone else's, evolved over time. One might be right about one thing and yet very wrong about another. We cannot say, "James Madison believed …" without qualifying such a statement chronologically,

---

8   Washington, Farewell Address.

any more than we can find one coherent political philosophy among the founders.

The Madison who wrote Federalist no. 10 was a different Madison than the one who fought at the Constitutional Convention for a consolidated federal government, and different still than the one who teamed up with Jefferson to undermine the Washington Administration. This alteration was not because of abstraction but because of real world events that led him to rethink his views on liberty and order. John Adams in the 1770s was convinced that virtue sustained and created government, but by the 1790s he had grown so jaded he felt sure only government could inculcate virtue in the people. The same Jefferson who wrote of the rights to life, liberty, and the pursuit of happiness also was a slave-owning planter who would have thrown the country into a trans-Atlantic war that destroyed the union, the very precondition of the liberty he claimed to cherish. This would not have been "right reason in action," as was Washington's bid for neutrality and his explanation of it as rooted in piety and justice.[9]

Jefferson's ideas of the relationship of the federal government to the states and to the people bear a close resemblance to the principle of subsidiarity though Jefferson was, to say the least, no Catholic. He was, however, a man interested in truth, and when he happened upon it he could usually see it. Consequently, where CST is concerned, Jefferson often seems preferable to the Hamilton whose idea for a commercial society involved the centralization of power. True, Hamilton recognized, with Edmund Burke, that our love proceeds outward, from family to neighbor to country. But this was not too apparent in his policies.

Yet it was Hamilton who sought to free the creative spirit of Americans by liberating them from slavery and the myopic

---

[9] St. Thomas Aquinas, quoted in *Catechism of the Catholic Church*, no. 1806.

agrarianism of Jefferson by promoting a diverse, commercial society wherein freedom allows citizens to pursue their best interest unencumbered by government intrusion but secure from disorder and equal under the law.

So when it comes to ascertaining the views of the founders and critically ascertaining what a Christian can appropriate from them, we must view them as a group, *over time*: the small government of Jefferson, Hamilton's recognition of the benefits of a commercial society, the wisdom of Madison about the necessity of government, the widespread recognition of the inseparable link among God and liberty and virtue, and the proof offered by Washington that virtue could be practiced—and over all this the absolutely necessary recognition of a higher moral law.

This is a view that is built upon the exercise of the classical virtues, but one that recognizes that in a republican form of government where the people are sovereign, the Christian virtues of faith, hope, and charity are necessary to avoid a leap into the abyss of relativism that can bring only libertinism and oppression. Undergirding this among all the founders was the recognition dating to classical times that republics require a virtuous population to prosper and to endure. True, they disagreed about how much virtue they could expect from the population. They disagreed, too, on what government ought to do or avoid doing to engender virtue in the population. But they understood well the link among virtue, freedom, and prosperity. As John Adams told Thomas Jefferson in 1813, "the general principles, on which the fathers achieved independence" were unalterable and part of human nature. These were "the general principles of Christianity ... and the general principles of English and American liberty."[10]

---

[10] John Adams to Thomas Jefferson, 28 June 1813, in *The Papers of Thomas Jefferson, Retirement Series*, ed. J. Jefferson Looney (Princeton: Princeton University Press, 2009), 6: 236–39.

Conclusion

The Catholic English historian Christopher Dawson thought Western Civilization was already well into its demise in the early twentieth century. Christendom—the unified Christian culture of the high middle ages that had taken one thousand years to form and flower—was long gone. What would take its place, Dawson wondered? In 1931 one of Dawson's contemporaries, T. S. Eliot, similarly ruminated on the future of Christian culture. The world, Eliot wrote, is "attempting to form a civilized but non-Christian mentality. The experiment will fail; but we must be very patient in awaiting its collapse; meanwhile redeeming the time: so that the faith may be preserved alive through the dark ages before us; to renew and rebuild civilization and save the World from suicide."[1]

In calling on Christians to "redeem the time," Eliot was quoting the fifth chapter of St. Paul's Letter to the Ephesians:

> For you were heretofore darkness, but now light in the Lord. Walk then as children of the light. For the fruit of the light is in all goodness, and justice, and truth; Proving what is well pleasing to God: And have no fellowship with the unfruitful works of darkness, but rather reprove

---

[1] T. S. Eliot, *Thoughts After Lambeth* (London: Faber and Faber, 1931).

> them. For the things that are done by them in secret, it is
> a shame even to speak of. But all things that are reproved,
> are made manifest by the light; for all that is made mani-
> fest is light. Wherefore he saith: Rise thou that sleepest,
> and arise from the dead: and Christ shall enlighten thee.
> See therefore, brethren, how you walk circumspectly: not
> as unwise, But as wise: redeeming the time, because the
> days are evil. (Eph. 5:8–16, Douay-Reims)

This is precisely the question Catholics must ask in any age: What is needed to redeem the time?

Is the American experiment so intrinsically incompatible with Catholic social teaching that Catholics should wash their hands of it and shake its dust from their feet? Is redeeming the time a waste of time for Catholic Americans? Dawson, who spent several years in the United States while teaching at Harvard University, did not think so. Despite "the pressure of secularization," he wrote in 1961, "at the same time America still possesses the priceless advantages of educational and intellectual freedom, so that we are still free to work and plan for the restoration of Christian culture." America, Dawson believed, held "the best prospect for the development of a Catholic culture" because of the combination of freedom, democracy, and "a much richer cultural inheritance than anything that American Protestants knew." Catholics were uniquely poised to "engage their nation's norms without capitulating to currently-prevalent secularism."[2] As Adam Schwartz points out, after World War II a whole host of English authors and critics were condemnatory of American culture, ranging from J. R. R. Tolkien to Graham Greene. "That Dawson was willing to break with these traditions shows, as Chesterton's similar willingness had, the extent of both his

---

2   Christopher Dawson, quoted in Adam Schwartz, "What They
    Saw in America: G. K. Chesterton's and Christopher Dawson's
    Views of the United States," *Faith and Reason* 28:1 (2003), 23–52.

anxieties about totalitarianism and his faith in Catholicism's transformative power."[3]

The American experience and the development of the Church's social doctrine since *Rerum Novarum*, particularly at the Second Vatican Council and during the papacy of John Paul II, corroborate Dawson's optimism. Yet there is a growing tendency among otherwise conservative Catholics to regard the American experiment not only as doomed to fail but to find in liberal democracy so much that is intrinsically contrary to the faith that a Catholic in good conscience must forswear the whole American project.

America, as G. K. Chesterton pointed out, is indeed beholden to some big ideas, ideas that have been elaborated on or abused or rejected over the past 240 years. But this is not the same as a "founding" if by that we mean a fashioning out of whole cloth a new nation based on liberal democracy as defined by a small group of men detached from history and wholly shaped by those Enlightenment ideals contrary to the classical and Christian heritage of Western civilization.

There were founders, and this book has evaluated some of them at length. When ideas of human freedom were codified by Americans, they tended to be rooted in the Christian view of the person as intrinsically dignified with a right to life and liberty. America may be "a country with a creed," as Chesterton said, but it was and is much more than that. As it turns out, Chesterton noticed this, too: "The real quality of America is much more subtle and complex than this; and is mixed not only of good and bad, and rational and mystical, but also of old and new. This is what makes the task of tracing the true proportions of American life so interesting and so impossible."[4]

3   Schwartz, "What They Saw in America."

4   Chesterton, *What I Saw in America*, xxx.

Chesterton thus recognized, as did Russell Kirk later, that the best America was the one that Americans had "built better than they knew." This was no creedal country in the sense of having an ideological blueprint such that if there was some anthropological error in the blueprint the whole edifice would crumble. This was the fruit of human experience, for good and ill, with both great promise and great peril. Chesterton noted as much:

> So far as that democracy becomes or remains Catholic and Christian, that democracy will remain democratic. In so far as it does not, it will become wildly and wickedly undemocratic. Its rich will riot with brutal indifference far beyond the feeble feudalism which retains some shadow of responsibility or at least of patronage. Its wage slaves will either sink into heathen slavery, or seek relief in theories that are destructive not only in method but in aim; since they are but the negations of the human appetites of property and personality. Eighteenth-century ideals, formulated in eighteenth-century language, have no longer in themselves the power to hold all these pagan passions back.... Men will more and more realise that there is no meaning in democracy if there is no meaning in anything; and that there is no meaning in anything if the universe has not a centre of significance and an authority that is the author of our rights.[5]

In this sense, the "creed" turns out to be a creed, but not a particularly eighteenth-century English one nor an ideological dogma, at least not at its roots. Its foundation, rather, as Kirk demonstrates in *Roots of American Order*, lies in the classical and Christian heritage of the West.

The ancients and medievals are not poster children for authentic self-government, the practice of virtue, the proper

---

[5] Chesterton, *What I Saw in America*, 263.

exercise of liberty, and the balance of the individual with the community, even if they promoted these ideas. We ought not be too nostalgic for their age. We certainly would not say that Roman Catholicism is incompatible with monarchy or aristocracy because of the failures of monarchs, any more than we would argue that Roman Catholicism is incompatible with the papacy due to the grim machinations and personal infidelities of certain popes. One fundamental point of CST is that "the coming of the Kingdom of God cannot be discerned in the perspective of a determined and definitive social, economic, or political organization."[6] Nor does the Church offer a one-size-fits-all social democratic blueprint. In the words of John Paul II, "Since it is not an ideology, the Christian faith does not presume to imprison changing socio-political realities in a rigid schema, and it recognizes that human life is realized in history in conditions that are diverse and imperfect." Furthermore, he concluded, "in constantly reaffirming the transcendent dignity of the person, the Church's method is always that of respect for freedom."[7] America's Catholic critics need to recognize that the only authentic instantiation of the kingdom of God is heaven. All else is to be sanctified and transformed by Catholics, working with and trying to expand what is well and good.

If the kingdom of heaven is not predicated on a definitive political organization, where do we find the kingdom on earth? We find it, according to the *Compendium*, "in the development of a human social sense which for mankind is a leaven for attaining wholeness, justice, and solidarity in openness to the Transcendent as a point of reference for one's own personal definitive fulfillment."[8] Has the American experiment allowed us to do this? Certainly it prefigured the Second Vatican Council

---

6 *Compendium of the Social Doctrine*, no. 51.

7 John Paul II, *Centesimus Annus*, no. 46.

8 *Compendium of the Social Doctrine*, no. 51.

in terms of religious freedom and the recognition, expanded over time, that while religious freedom can indeed mask religious indifference, the latter is not the inevitable product of the former. The former, however, is required by the authentic understanding of the free human person contained in CST. Americans, for good and for ill, have over their history been among the least indifferent people when it comes to religion and the appeal "to the Transcendent as a point of reference."

Catholic social teaching since the 1890s has grown in its recognition of the importance of democracy as it has promoted solidarity and recognized in participation the most prominent fruit of subsidiarity. Due to modern conditions, CST seems weighted toward democracy, not against it. Again, as the *Compendium* points out innumerable times, CST responds to new events and developments by applying the deposit of faith and Catholic principles. By comparison to the anti-religious European liberalism of the nineteenth century, America becomes the positive test case for religious freedom and liberty more generally. America continues to be more deeply religious than any other western country or any country that once was part of Christendom or remains a confessional state. Only of late has the United States become sucked into the morass of post-Christendom and radically secular progressivism. This current state of affairs cries out for sanctification, redemption, and restoration, not despair and abandonment.[9]

So CST seems to be saying not just that liberal democracy is compatible with Roman Catholicism insofar as any political economy can be, but that at this moment it is the most compatible in light of "the complex events that mark our time."

---

[9] See, for example, Samuel Gregg, *Becoming Europe: Economic Decline, Culture, and How American Can Avoid a European Future* (New York: Encounter, 2013); and Francis Cardinal George, *The Difference God Makes.*

These complex events are the peculiar challenges of modernity, globalism, and industrialization.[10] In the face of these, "the Church values the democratic system inasmuch as it ensures the participation of citizens in making political choices, guarantees to the governed the possibility both of electing and holding accountable those who govern them, and of replacing them through peaceful means when appropriate."[11]

Our brief consideration of America's founding demonstrates that the long American project is in large measure compatible with Roman Catholic teaching. To say Catholicism is inimical to republicanism is to misunderstand both. It is to misunderstand republicanism as an ontologically singular thing based on a blueprint written by Publius and Locke. Likewise, it is to misunderstand Roman Catholic teaching as unable to respond "with new strategies suited to the demands of our time and in keeping with human needs and resources."[12] It also is to forget that the Church, in her social doctrine, "does not attempt to structure or organize society, but to appeal to, guide, and form consciences."[13] We ought not embalm Catholic teaching in those moments of the nineteenth century that so clearly demand historical contextualization, such as when Popes Gregory XVI and Pius IX condemned liberalism or denounced "Americanism." John Paul II rightly notes in *Centesimus Annus* that, "The Church respects the legitimate autonomy of the democratic order and is not entitled to express preferences for this or that institutional or constitutional solution. Her contribution to the political order is precisely her vision of the dignity of the person revealed in all its fullness in the mystery of the Incarnate Word."[14]

---

10 *Compendium of the Social Doctrine*, no. 10.

11 John Paul II, *Centesimus Annus*, no. 46.

12 *Compendium of the Social Doctrine*, no. 10.

13 *Compendium of the Social Doctrine*, no. 81.

14 John Paul II, *Centesimus Annus*, no. 47.

Was the United States built on a creed? Yes, in a sense, but creeds are symbols of deeper beliefs. The American creed was never an ideology pregnant with inevitable failure. Chesterton recognized this, as did John Paul II. Catholic critics of American democracy should recognize it as well so that people of good will might redeem the time in a manner suited to our time.

References

Church Documents

Unless otherwise noted, Church documents are available at www
.vatican.va.

Catechism of the Catholic Church (1993).

Pontifical Council for Justice and Peace, *Compendium of the Social
Doctrine of the Church* (2004).

Pope Benedict XVI. *Ad limina* address to bishops of the United States,
19 January 2012.

Pope Gregory XVI, Encyclical Letter *Mirari Vos* (1832), http://www
.papalencyclicals.net/greg16/g16mirar.htm.

Pope John Paul II. Encyclical Letter *Centesimus Annus* (1991).

Pope John Paul II, Homily at Camden Yards, Baltimore, Maryland,
8 October 1995.

Pope Pius IX, *Syllabus of Errors* (1864), https://www.ewtn.com/library
/papaldoc/p9syll.htm.

Second Vatican Council, Declaration on Religious Liberty (*Dignitatis
Humanae*).

United States Conference of Catholic Bishops. "Seven Themes of
Catholic Social Teaching," http://www.usccb.org/beliefs-and-
teachings/what-we-believe/catholic-social-teaching/seven-themes-
of-catholic-social-teaching.cfm.

United States Conference of Catholic Bishops Ad Hoc Committee on Religious Liberty. "Our First, Most Cherished Liberty: A Statement on Religious Liberty," 2012, http://www.usccb.org/issues-and-action/religious-liberty/our-first-most-cherished-liberty.cfm.

Other Sources

Acton, Lord. "The Church in the Modern World." In *Essays in Religion, Politics, and Morality*, vol. 3. Edited by J. Rufus Fears. Indianapolis: Liberty Classics, 1985.

Adams, John. "Thoughts on Government" (1776). In *The Portable John Adams*. Edited by John Patrick Diggins. New York: Penguin Books, 2004.

Allen, William B. "Radical Challenges to Liberal Democracy." In *Toward the Renewal of Civilization*. Edited by T. William Boxx and Gary M. Quinlivan. Grand Rapids: Eerdmans, 1998.

Altholz, Joseph L., Damian McElrath, and James C. Holland, eds. *The Correspondence of Lord Acton and Richard Simpson*, 3 vols., London: Cambridge University Press, 1978.

Aquinas, Thomas. *Summa Theologiae*.

Augustine of Hippo. *City of God*, https://www.ccel.org/ccel/schaff/npnf102.iv.XIX.17.html.

Burke, Edmund. Speech to Parliament, 22 March 1775. In *The Works of the Right Honourable Edmund Burke*. 6 vols. London: Henry G. Bohn, 1854–1856.

Burnett, Edmund Cody, ed. *Letters of Members of the Continental Congress*. Carnegie Institution of Washington, 1921.

Brownson, Orestes. *The American Republic*. Detroit: H. F. Brownson, 1905.

Carey, Patrick W. *Orestes Brownson: American Religious Weathervane*. Grand Rapids: Eerdmans, 2004.

Chesterton, G. K. *What I Saw in America*. New York: Dodd, Mead, and Co., 1922. Reprint, G. K. Chesterton: *Collected Works*, 37 vols. San Francisco: Ignatius Press, 1990.

Conrad, Stephen A. "Putting Rights Talk in Its Place: *The Summary View* Revisited." In *Jeffersonian Legacies*. Edited by Peter S. Onuf. Charlottesville: University of Virginia Press, 1993.

Deneen, Patrick. *Why Liberalism Failed*. New Haven and London: Yale University Press, 2018.

Dickinson, John. 13 August 1787, Constitutional Convention, Madison Debates, http://avalon.law.yale.edu/18th_century/debates_813.asp.

Eliot, T. S. *Thoughts After Lambeth*. London: Faber and Faber, 1931.

George, Frances Cardinal. *The Difference God Makes: A Catholic Vision of Faith, Communion, and Culture*. New York: Crossroad Publishing Company, 2009.

Goldman, Samuel. "The Inevitability of Liberal Failure?" *University Bookman* (January 15, 2018), www.kirkcenter.org/bookman/article/the-inevitability-of-liberal-failure.

Gregg, Samuel. *Becoming Europe: Economic Decline, Culture, and How America Can Avoid a European Future*. New York: Encounter, 2013.

Henry, Patrick. Speech at the Second Virginia Convention, 23 March 1775, St. John's Church, Richmond, Virginia.

Henry, Patrick, to James Monroe, 24 January 1791. In *The Papers of James Monroe*. Edited by Daniel Preston. Westport: Greenwood Press, 2006.

Jefferson, Thomas. *Notes on the State of Virginia* (1787). Documenting the American South, https://docsouth.unc.edu/southlit/jefferson/jefferson.html.

Jefferson, Thomas, to Henry Lee, 8 May 1825. In *Thomas Jefferson: Writings*. Edited by Merrill D. Peterson. New York: Library of America, 1984.

Jefferson, Thomas, to Isaac H. Tiffany, 4 April 1819, https://founders.archives.gov/documents/Jefferson/98-01-02-0303.

Jefferson, Thomas, to John Adams, 11 April 1823. *Morals of Jesus*. Edited by Dickinson W. Adams, Ruth W. Lester, and Eugene R. Sheridan. Princeton: Princeton University Press, 1983.

Jefferson, Thomas, to Timothy Pickering, 27 February 1821. In *Jefferson's Extracts from the Gospels: "The Philosophy of Jesus" and "The Life and Morals of Jesus"*. Edited by Dickinson W. Adams, Ruth W. Lester, and Eugene R. Sheridan. Princeton: Princeton University Press, 1983. 403.

Jefferson, Thomas, to William Short, 3 January 1793, https://founders.archives.gov/documents/Jefferson/01-25-02-0016.

Kidd, Thomas S. *God of Liberty: A Religious History of the American Revolution*. New York: Basic Books, 2010.

King, Jr., Martin Luther. "Letter from a Birmingham Jail" (16 April 1963). African Studies Center, University of Pennsylvania, https://www.africa.upenn.edu/Articles_Gen/Letter_Birmingham.html.

Kirk, Russell. *The American Cause*. Regnery, 1957; reprint, Wilmington, Delaware: Intercollegiate Studies Institute, 2002.

Kirk, Russell. "Orestes Brownson and the Just Society." In *The Essential Russell Kirk: Selected Essays*. Edited by George A. Panichas. Wilmington: ISI Books, 2007.

Kirk, Russell. *The Roots of American Order*. 1974; reprint, Wilmington: ISI Books, 2003.

Looney, J. Jefferson, ed. *The Papers of Thomas Jefferson, Retirement Series*. Princeton: Princeton University Press, 2009.

Murray, John Courtney. *We Hold These Truths: Catholic Reflections on the American Proposition*. Kansas City: Sheed and Ward, 1960.

Noll, Mark. *America's God: From Jonathan Edwards to Abraham Lincoln*. Oxford: Oxford University Press, 2005.

Pidluzny, Jonathan W., and Murray S. Y. Bessette. "Avarice and Ambition in America: The Founders' Debate on the Political Place of the Selfish Passions in the Constitutional Order of the United States." *Journal of Markets & Morality* 22, no. 1 (Spring 2019): 117–46.

Pinheiro, John C. *Missionaries of Republicanism: A Religious History of the Mexican-American War*. Oxford: Oxford University Press, 2014.

Robespierre, Maximilien. *Report upon the Principles of Political Morality which Are to Form the Basis of the Administration of the Interior Concerns of the Republic*. Philadelphia, 1794.

Schwartz, Adam. "What They Saw in America: G. K. Chesterton's and Christopher Dawson's Views of the United States." *Faith and Reason* 28, no. 1 (2003): 23–52.

Stoner, James R., Jr. *Common Law and Liberal Theory: Coke, Hobbes, and the Origins of American Constitutionalism*. Lawrence: University of Kansas Press, 1992.

Tocqueville, Alexis de. *Democracy in America* (1835–1840). Translated by Gerald E. Bevan. New York: Penguin Books, 2003.

Tocqueville, Alexis de. *The Old Regime and the Revolution* (1856). Translated by John Bonner. New York: Harper & Brothers, https://oll.libertyfund.org/titles/2419#de-Tocqueville_1597_591.

Washington, George. Farewell Address, 19 September 1796, http://gwpapers.virginia.edu/documents_gw/farewell/transcript.html.

Washington, George, to Henry Laurens, 14 November 1778. *The Writings of George Washington* 39 vols. Edited by John C. Fitzpatrick. Washington: U.S. Government Printing Office, 1931–1934, 13:254–57.

Washington, George, to John Hancock, 25 September 1776. In *The Papers of George Washington*. Edited by Philander D. Chase and Frank E. Grizzard, Jr. Revolutionary War Series. Charlottesville: University Press of Virginia, 1994, 6:393–401.

Whitney, Gleaves. "Afterword." In Russell Kirk, *The American Cause*. Regnery. 1957; reprint, Wilmington, Delaware: Intercollegiate Studies Institute, 2002.

Wilken, Robert Louis. *Liberty in the Things of God: The Christian Origins of Religious Freedom*. New Haven: Yale University Press, 2019.

Winship, Michael. *Godly Republicanism: Puritans, Pilgrims, and a City on a Hill*. Cambridge: Harvard University Press, 2012.

Winthrop, John. "On Liberty." Speech before the General Court of Massachusetts (1645), http://www.constitution.org/bcp/winthlib.htm.

About the Author

JOHN C. PINHEIRO (PhD, University of Tennessee) is professor of history and the founding director of Catholic Studies at Aquinas College in Grand Rapids, Michigan, where he also cofounded the Semester-in-Rome. Prior to joining the Aquinas faculty in 2004 he was assistant editor on the Presidential Series of the *Papers of George Washington* at the University of Virginia. Dr. Pinheiro also is the consulting editor on James K. Polk for the American President Resource at the University of Virginia's Miller Center of Public Affairs. He is the author of books and articles on the early American republic, including the award-winning *Missionaries of Republicanism: A Religious History of the Mexican-American War* (Oxford University Press, 2014).